CONTENTS

INTRODUCTION

This book is for anyone who loves cooking and wants to learn a little more. It's the sequel to *Rosemary Shrager's Absolutely Foolproof Classic Home Cooking*, which concentrates on basic techniques – the skills you need to know for everyday cooking. This second volume focuses on the kind of cooking that you don't do every day – dishes for large gatherings of family and friends, for special occasions or for using up a glut of produce in season. It is a celebration of traditional skills, such as making a consommé or raised pie or curing a leg of ham. Each technique is accompanied by step-by-step photography and instructions to help you master the dish, along with advice and tips on how to achieve perfect results every time.

The technique recipes are not quick after-work suppers (although if that's what you are looking for, you will find plenty of other dishes here to fit the bill). They are projects, to be tackled at the weekend, perhaps, when you have more time. They need a certain amount of planning and forethought, but it is well worth it because you will then have a wonderful stash of homemade food in your fridge and it will be much better – and cheaper – than anything you can buy.

Some of the recipes serve quite a lot of people, but if you are making a celebratory dish it's important to be generous. And when you undertake a cooking project such as curing meat or fish, there's no point doing things by halves. Dishes such as the Galantine of Chicken (see page 38) make superb leftovers, which will keep for several days in the fridge, and home-cured meat or fish will go a long way. The point is, not to waste any food. That is one of the reasons I'm so keen for people to learn cookery techniques rather than just follow recipes. If you are no longer tied to recipes but have the confidence to create your own dishes, you will never have to throw food out again. A leftover chicken, for example, can be used to make rissoles, a pilaf, a ravioli filling, a consommé, a soup, a casserole or a risotto. In my family, we have something called splodge pie, where we layer all the leftover vegetables in a dish with a little butter and some herbs, pour over some stock and bake slowly till tender, then cover with pastry or cheese and bake again. It's thrifty and delicious.

What I hope this book and the previous one will do is make sure you are not frightened of dealing with food but instead feel ready to tackle anything.

I will hold up my hands and admit that you will have to think about it a little more than you might be accustomed to doing, but the rewards of taking control of the food you eat are immense. It's very satisfying to master a new technique and then use it to create your own dishes, based on what you have in the storecupboard or fridge. If you are following a recipe, you can be left high and dry if you can't get all the ingredients you need. Learning culinary skills means you will always be able to adapt to what's available.

The best way to ensure that cooking is fun and not a chore is to allow yourself plenty of time, particularly when you attempt a new recipe. Break the recipes down where possible and do a little bit here and a little bit there. Some of the recipes featured in this book consist of several elements, but they are not intrinsically difficult and if you tackle each element separately everything becomes much easier to manage. Take your time, plan well and spread the workload over a day or two. When you are entertaining, this is a much safer and less stressful way of cooking than choosing a recipe where everything has to be cooked at the last minute.

It's impossible to include everything in one book, so I have concentrated on the techniques that I think are especially relevant today. Some of them might surprise you – consommés, for example, are no longer featured regularly on restaurant menus. But they are so satisfying to make, and they turn something quite ordinary into something special, transforming a simple, well-flavoured stock into a sparkling-clear liquid. They also deserve their place in the book because they are so thrifty – you can buy bones from the butcher to make the stock very cheaply and you need only a small amount of garnish.

In fact, quite a few dishes that we pay a lot for in restaurants are really economical to make at home. Ravioli, for example, is a classic Italian way of using up scraps, while duck confit is a means of preserving a relatively cheap cut of meat – the leg rather than the more expensive breast. There is a lot of game in this book, which can be pricy, but if you buy it in season it is very good value and it's a chance to make some wonderful classic dishes.

The Salmon en Croûte (see page 168) and Glazed Cured Ham (see page 130) may take a while to prepare, but they are such delightful dishes that I couldn't resist sharing them with you. When you want to cook something special, for a feast or celebration, these are the recipes you should turn to.

On my cookery courses, people ask me all sorts of questions and I never feel that a question is too much or too silly. Many of the tips and ideas that follow the step-by-step recipes in this book are in response to these questions. I hope they will help you have confidence in the kitchen, so that you can move your cooking up a level and experience the pleasure of real cooking: turning out a beautifully crafted raised pie, making your own sausages or boiling and dressing a lovely fresh crab.

I wrote this book because it is what I would have liked myself when I was learning to cook. I picked up my knowledge here and there, reading, experimenting and being fortunate enough to work with some wonderful chefs. But I can honestly say that it would have been so much easier if a book like this one had been around, so that all the things I needed to know were in one place. I hope you will find it an invaluable resource for learning new skills and getting maximum enjoyment out of cooking and eating.

NOTES ON THE RECIPES

■ All spoon measures are level unless otherwise stated.

■ All eggs are large unless otherwise stated. I much prefer to use good free-range eggs for the best colour and flavour.

■ I recommend fine sea salt for dressings, salads and cold dishes and in bread making. Otherwise I use ordinary flaky sea salt.

■ Pepper should always be freshly ground. I use white pepper when I don't want to see the black grains in a dish but I do use black whenever I can, as I prefer the flavour.

■ I favour unsalted butter, as I like to add my own salt to a dish and I find I can control the flavour better in this way.

■ I use organic flour from a local mill, Sunflours, near Ripon in North Yorkshire. I recommend you seek out a good local flour if possible, as it makes all the difference to your baking.

■ It is very important to buy a good set of knives. For me, they are the tools of my trade. I use Wustof knives, as they handle well and have a good weight.

■ A surprisingly useful piece of kitchen equipment is a flexible paint scraper. I bought one 35 years ago and use it like a palette knife. I call it my swish, and if I lost it I would probably have to give up work.

CONVERSION CHARTS

OVEN TEMPERATURES

°C	°C (fan)	°F	Gas mark
110°C	90°C	225°F	¼
120°C	100°C	250°F	½
140°C	120°C	275°F	1
150°C	130°C	300°F	2
160°C	140°C	325°F	3
180°C	160°C	350°F	4
190°C	170°C	375°F	5
200°C	180°C	400°F	6
220°C	200°C	425°F	7
230°C	210°C	450°F	8
240°C	220°C	475°F	9

SPOONS

1 teaspoon = one 5ml spoon
1 tablespoon = one 15ml spoon

WEIGHTS

5g	¼oz
15g	½oz
20g	¾oz
25g	1oz
50g	2oz
75g	3oz
125g	4oz
150g	5oz
175g	6oz
200g	7oz
250g	8oz
275g	9oz
300g	10oz
325g	11oz
375g	12oz
400g	13oz
425g	14oz
475g	15oz
500g	1lb
625g	1¼lb
750g	1½lb
875g	1¾lb
1kg	2lb
1.25kg	2½lb
1.5kg	3lb
1.75kg	3½lb
2kg	4lb

VOLUME

15ml	½ fl oz
25ml	1 fl oz
50ml	2 fl oz
75ml	3 fl oz
100ml	3½ fl oz
125ml	4 fl oz
150ml	¼ pint
175ml	6 fl oz
200ml	7 fl oz
250ml	8 fl oz
275ml	9 fl oz
300ml	½ pint
325ml	11 fl oz
350ml	12 fl oz
375ml	13 fl oz
400ml	14 fl oz
450ml	¾ pint
475ml	16 fl oz
500ml	17 fl oz
575ml	18 fl oz
600ml	1 pint
750ml	1¼ pints
900ml	1½ pints
1 litre	1¾ pints
1.2 litres	2 pints
1.5 litres	2½ pints
1.8 litres	3 pints
2 litres	3½ pints
2.5 litres	4 pints

MEASUREMENTS

2.5mm	⅛ inch
5mm	¼ inch
1cm	½ inch
2cm	¾ inch
2.5cm	1 inch
5cm	2 inches
7cm	3 inches
10cm	4 inches
12cm	5 inches
15cm	6 inches
18cm	7 inches
20cm	8 inches
23cm	9 inches
25cm	10 inches
28cm	11 inches
30cm	12 inches

EQUIPMENT

If you have the right equipment in the kitchen, it will make your life so much easier. You don't need a lot of gadgets in order to cook well but there are a few items that are indispensable. Good-quality kitchenware will last a lifetime, so it's well worth the investment.

GENERAL KITCHEN EQUIPMENT

My advice when stocking up on kitchen equipment is to buy just one piece at a time but make it the best you can afford. You really don't need much to begin with: pans, ovenproof dishes, sieves, good knives and a selection of spoons and other utensils.

The saucepans you use are very important. Decide which range you prefer and then gradually build up a collection if you can't afford to splash out all at once. I favour stainless-steel pans with a good, heavy base. Unlike cheaper pans, they don't get hot spots and cook unevenly, neither do they buckle on the hob. It's useful to have a selection of casseroles and gratin dishes, too. The coloured, cast-iron ones are very sturdy to cook in and are attractive enough to take straight to the table.

Scales are essential in the kitchen. My favourite are Salter electronic scales, because you can put your mixing bowl straight on to them for weighing the ingredients. I also find fine-meshed sieves indispensible. A chinois, or conical sieve, is very handy, too, for straining sauces, soups and purées so that they are really smooth.

I use tongs for absolutely everything in the kitchen – once you acquire them, you'll wonder how you ever managed without. I have come to rely on microplane graters for Parmesan, fresh ginger and citrus zest, but also keep an old-fashioned box grater for other cheeses. If you cook a lot of fish, proper fish tweezers with a flat base save a lot of frustration when trying to remove bones. For joints of roast meat, a meat thermometer is a failsafe way of checking whether they are cooked to your liking. Finally, a freestanding electric mixer is a big investment but it does earn its keep, as it's a great all-in-one piece of kit.

EQUIPMENT

Casserole

Steamer

Colander

Terrine

Whisk

Frying pan

Chinois

Sauté pan

Graters

Gratin dish

Sieve

Tongs

Chopping board

Pasta machine

Piping bag

Food mixer

Thermometer

Scales

Needles

Potato ricer

Fish tweezers

Timer

Scissors

Meat thermometer

KNIVES

Knives are the tools of a cook's trade. They are an expensive investment but once you've bought them you have them for life – if you look after them. Your first purchase should be a knife sharpener, as if you don't keep knives sharp there is no point in having them. I find a steel more effective than a whetstone. Choose a knife that feels good in your hand – it should be a comfortable weight for you. When shopping for knives, I always take a potato with me and ask if I can test the knife out on it. The best knives are made of one solid piece of stainless steel that runs right through the handle; they last for much longer.

The knife you will use most is a cook's knife, a large, straight knife with a wide blade about 18–20cm long. It should be wide enough for your knuckles not to touch the work surface as you chop. It's important to use the right knife for the job, as it makes your task so much easier. A fish filleting knife has a fine, flexible blade that enables you to sweep against the bones of the fish. A large serrated knife can be a great all-rounder, suitable for cutting virtually anything. A cleaver is the correct tool for chopping up meat bones or cutting off knuckles; if you use your ordinary knives for this you will ruin them. A paring knife is useful for cutting round curved items such as citrus fruit or for removing the core from a pear. A boning knife has a fine tip at the top, which helps you manoeuvre it around the bone. A turning or peeling knife has a curved blade and is ideal for peeling or shaping fruit and vegetables. An oriental santoku knife can be used for everything – if I were to be restricted to just one knife, this is the one I would probably choose. Finally, a carving knife is ideal for slicing cuts of meat.

Don't keep sharp knives loose in a drawer: first, you can cut yourself and secondly, it doesn't do them any good to be thrown in a drawer as they can become dulled or chipped. Keep them either in a knife block or on a magnetic strip on the wall.

Knife sharpening

Hold the steel tightly in one hand and the knife in the other. Starting at the base of the steel, hold the knife blade at a 12-degree angle away from the steel and draw it along the shaft until you reach the point. Then take the knife under the steel and repeat the process with the blade against the underside of the steel. Repeat 6–8 times.

Knife safety

Sharp knives are safer than blunt ones, as they are less likely to slip. Always cut on a flat surface and hold the food firmly with your other hand, tucking your fingers under as you cut, with your knuckles facing the knife.

Fish filleting knife

Large serrated knife

Cleaver

Straight paring knife

Boning knife

Turning or peeling knife

Oriental santoku knife

Cook's knife

Carving knife

CHOPPING AND SLICING

The first thing chefs have to learn is how to slice and dice vegetables properly. Obviously at home you don't need to go to the extremes of a professional chef but it's a useful skill to master.

When you cut vegetables, think about whether they are just for flavouring or will be an important visual element in the finished dish. If they are just for flavouring, you can chop them quite roughly; this is called a mirepoix. If they will be part of the presentation, they should be much neater. Below are some examples of the different shapes in which vegetables can be cut and the names that chefs use to describe them.

A large knife is best for chopping and slicing. It might feel uncomfortable at first but stick with it, as it is much more efficient. For very fine dicing, however, such as the brunoise below, a small knife is more practical. Ideally, you should sharpen your knife on a steel before each use. A sharp knife will give good clean pieces, which look better and cook more evenly.

To chop or slice, hold the vegetable firmly with one hand on a chopping board with your fingers tucked under, out of the way of the blade. Hold the knife in your other hand, just above the vegetable with the point on the board. Push the knife down and forward, cutting as you do so, then bring it up and back with a rocking motion to make the next cut. The less you lift the knife off the board, the quicker you can cut. Take it slowly at first though, until you have got the technique right; speed can come later. Opposite are examples of a few different vegetable preparation techniques.

Baton

A baton is a square stick. Slim batons are useful for stir-fries, larger ones for roasting or casseroles.

Brunoise

Brunoise is a very fine dice of about 2mm, useful for stuffings or garnishes.

Fine julienne

Fine julienne are very thin strips about 1.5mm thick. Make fine julienne of vegetables to use in salads.

Large julienne

Large julienne are thin strips about 3mm thick; they can be sautéed in a little butter.

Large dice

Large dice are cubes with sides measuring about 1cm; they work well in casseroles and soups.

Small dice

Small dice are cubes with sides measuring about 5mm; they look good in the final presentation of a dish.

Deseeding and dicing tomatoes

1 Cut each tomato into quarters, removing the core if large.

2 Run a paring knife between the flesh and the seeds to remove the seeds from the tomato and discard.

3 Using a cook's knife, chop the tomato flesh into dice.

Slicing leafy greens

1 Cut out the hard white core from each leaf.

2 Roll up the leaves tightly; you can do them individually or roll a few at a time.

3 With a cook's knife, cut across the rolled-up leaves to create ribbons.

Slicing onions into half rings

1 Using a cook's knife, cut the unpeeled onion in half through the root.

2 Peel off the skin, leaving the root attached.

3 With the onion cut-side down on a board, slice across, discarding the root.

Preparing parsnips

1 Using a cook's knife, trim the top and bottom from the parsnip.

2 Peel the parsnip down its length.

3 Chop it into quarters, cutting out the core if the parsnip is large and woody.

VEGETABLES

This chapter includes plenty of recipes for different types of vegetables and I hope it will encourage you to eat more vegetables and try new dishes. Understanding how to prepare and cook vegetables enhances the pleasure of eating them. Recognising which parts of each vegetable you can eat is important, too. A lot of people throw away the stalks of broccoli, for example, but I like to peel them and cut them into fine strips to use in stir-fries. Seasonal treats such as baby artichokes and asparagus are an absolute delight, and preparing them properly ensures you preserve their lovely texture and flavour.

The vegetables are cooked in boiling water, then covered in olive oil so they become meltingly tender and delicious. If you can't get baby artichokes you can use large ones instead — but remember to adjust the cooking time according to size. Once prepared, you can store these in the fridge for several days.

BABY ARTICHOKES
in olive oil

To prepare the baby artichokes, follow steps 1 to 4

SERVES 4

8 baby globe artichokes

juice of 2 lemons

extra virgin olive oil for coating

2 bay leaves

2 garlic cloves, thinly sliced

fine sea salt and black pepper

1 First prepare the artichokes. Peel the stalks with a potato peeler.

2 Remove some of the leaves on the outside of the artichokes to expose the paler leaves.

3 Trim off the top of each artichoke and discard the tips of the leaves.

4 Put the artichokes into cold water into which you have squeezed the juice of 1 lemon, to prevent discolouring.

5 Cook the artichokes in a large saucepan of boiling water for 4–5 minutes, or until a knife inserted into the base comes out easily.

6 If they are a little on the large side, cook for a few minutes longer.

7 Drain the artichokes thoroughly. Cut them in half lengthways and put them into a bowl.

8 While they are still warm, coat liberally with olive oil.

9 Add the remaining lemon juice, bay leaves and garlic and season with salt and pepper. Mix together well.

TIPS AND IDEAS

■ When buying artichokes, choose ones that don't look dry or withered and have tightly packed heads – a good indication of freshness. If possible, pull out a leaf from the centre; if it won't come out easily, the artichoke is stale.

■ Artichokes are best eaten fresh. Store them in the fridge for no more than 3 days.

■ Be sure to put the artichokes into lemony water straight away as you prepare them; they turn black very quickly. I tend to rub large artichokes with ½ lemon while I am preparing them.

■ To prepare large artichokes, cut off the stalk, then remove the lower leaves with scissors. Slice across the top of each artichoke to remove the tips. You can cook them in boiling water at this stage for 25–30 minutes, then use a spoon to scoop out the hairy choke from the centre and serve with melted butter or a vinaigrette for dipping the leaves into. Alternatively, prepare the artichokes fully before cooking by taking off all the leaves, then removing the flower (the choke) by pulling it away from the bottom with a teaspoon. Scrape the inside with the spoon so it is completely clean, then cut away the green left from the stalk at the base. Cut the artichokes into quarters and cook as in the main recipe.

■ When cooking artichokes that will be baked in a gratin, you need to boil them for a little longer; add a further 3–4 minutes to the cooking time.

■ Artichokes are very good roasted. Prepare as described above, then instead of boiling them, spread them out on a baking tray and drizzle with olive oil. Place in an oven preheated to 180°C/Gas Mark 4 and roast for 25–30 minutes, until tender.

■ Artichokes in oil make a lovely present, packed into a sterilised Kilner jar and topped up with more olive oil. To sterilise jars, wash the jars and lids thoroughly in very hot water, allow them to dry, then place in an oven preheated to 140°C/Gas Mark 1 for about 20 minutes. Remove and leave to cool for 10 minutes before filling them.

baby artichoke variations

Pasta with Artichokes – follow the recipe on pages 18–19, steps 1–7, then toss the artichokes with buttered cooked pasta, a handful of herbs (parsley and coriander are good), a generous squeeze of lemon juice and plenty of black pepper.

Artichokes in Cheese Sauce – follow the recipe on pages 18–19, steps 1–7, adding an extra 3–4 minutes to the cooking time. Then cover the artichokes in a cheesy béchamel sauce, scatter grated cheese on top, place in an oven preheated to 180°C/Gas Mark 4 and bake for 35 minutes, until browned and bubbling.

Artichoke and Tomato Gratin – follow the recipe on pages 18–19, steps 1–7, adding an extra 3–4 minutes to the cooking time. Then layer the artichokes in a gratin dish with sliced tomato and season well. Cover with grated Gruyère cheese, place in an oven preheated to 180°C/Gas Mark 4 and bake for 35 minutes, until the cheese is melted and lightly browned.

Artichokes with Coriander and Feta – follow the recipe on pages 18–19, adding 2 teaspoons of lightly crushed coriander seeds to the artichokes with the lemon, bay and garlic. Toss in 250g feta cheese, broken into chunks, and a handful of stoned black olives. Serve as a salad, with plenty of crusty bread to mop up the oily juices.

POTATO WEDGES WITH FRESH HERBS AND GARLIC

These are very simple to make but the trick is not to turn the potatoes too soon during cooking. It's an extremely pretty dish, with the lemon and bay leaves. For a colourful twist, you could gently heat the oil first and add a little saffron so the potatoes become a beautiful yellow.

Serves 8

1 rounded tablespoon rosemary leaves, plus 2 sprigs

1.5kg small, waxy potatoes

1 lemon, cut into 8 wedges

6 small bay leaves

3 garlic cloves, peeled but left whole

olive oil for coating

coarse sea salt

1 Pound the rosemary leaves in a mortar with a pestle. Cut the potatoes into wedges like large, blunt chips.

2 Combine the potatoes and pounded rosemary leaves with the lemon wedges, bay leaves, garlic cloves and rosemary sprigs on a roasting tray, then add enough oil to coat the potatoes and sprinkle with some coarse sea salt. Place in an oven preheated to 200°C/Gas Mark 6 and roast for 1 hour, until tender and golden, turning the potatoes over halfway through.

RÖSTI

If you make this in one big pan, it's a lovely sharing dish, or you could make individual rösti by putting metal rings in the frying pan and filling each with the mixture. I like rösti to be slightly caramelised and crisp on the outside.

Serves 4

500g all-purpose potatoes, such as Maris Piper

6 tablespoons clarified unsalted butter (see page 268, step 2)

½ onion, finely chopped

sea salt and black pepper

1 Cook the potatoes in their skins in a large saucepan of boiling water for about 10–15 minutes, until just cooked through. Drain well and leave to cool.

2 Meanwhile, heat 2 tablespoons of the clarified butter in a large, non-stick frying pan, add the onion and cook gently for at least 5 minutes, until softened. Remove from the pan and leave to cool.

3 Peel the cooled potatoes by scraping off the skins with a knife. Coarsely grate the potatoes, put them into a large bowl and season with salt and pepper. Add the onion and mix well.

4 Wipe the frying pan clean. Add 2 tablespoons of the remaining clarified butter, then add the potato mixture. Press down with a fish slice and cook gently on a medium-low heat for about 10–12 minutes, until golden brown underneath. Cover the pan with a large plate and invert the potato cake on to it. Add the remaining clarified butter to the pan, then slide the rösti back in and cook for a further 10 minutes or until golden brown on the second side. Cut into wedges to serve.

FONDANT POTATOES

Fondant potatoes are a classic dish, rich and delicious, and so delicious to eat. Just don't think of the calories!

Serves 6

6 large all-purpose potatoes, such as Maris Piper

100g unsalted butter

chicken stock

sea salt and black pepper

1 Peel the potatoes, then cut each of them into a cylinder shape. This can be done using a plain 5–6cm round cutter, then the sharp edges rounded off with a small knife. Alternatively, cut the potato into a rectangle and then round off the sides and top.

2 Choose a heavy-based saucepan in which the potatoes will just fit standing up. Melt the butter in it, then add the potatoes. Pour in enough stock to come halfway up the potatoes – you should have a mixture of half butter and half stock. Season with salt and pepper. Cook, uncovered, over a low-medium heat for 45 minutes, then turn the potatoes over and cook on the other side for about another 45 minutes, until very tender. The stock and butter will eventually evaporate to leave the potatoes with a golden, caramelised top.

BOULANGÈRE POTATOES

This traditional French dish makes a good alternative to dauphinoise potatoes if you want to avoid cream.

Serves 6

100g unsalted butter

500g onions, very thinly sliced

1.25kg all-purpose potatoes, such as Maris Piper, peeled and thinly sliced

2 garlic cloves, finely chopped

2 tablespoons thyme leaves

350ml vegetable stock

sea salt and black pepper

1 Melt 25g of the butter in a large frying pan, add the onions and cook over a medium heat for about 10 minutes, until pale golden.

2 Grease a 23cm round gratin dish with some of the remaining butter and arrange a layer of potato slices in it. Add a layer of onion with a scattering of the chopped garlic, a sprinkling of the thyme leaves and some of the stock. Repeat the layers, adding the remaining stock as you go. Finish with a layer of potatoes arranged in an attractive pattern. Dot the top with the remaining butter, then cover with foil.

3 Place in an oven preheated to 180°C/Gas Mark 4 and cook for about 1 hour or until the potatoes are tender, removing the foil 30 minutes before the end of the cooking time so that the top turns golden brown.

EXOTIC MUSHROOM CHILLI VODKA WITH HORSERADISH BLOODY MARYS

This is probably not what you'd expect to see in a vegetable chapter but it was just too good to leave out. A Chinese-inspired twist on a Bloody Mary, it has plenty of heat from the chilli, while the mushrooms give it a very earthy flavour. Warning: it's unbelievably potent.

Makes about 500ml flavoured vodka

20g mixed exotic mushrooms

750ml bottle of vodka (you will need 425ml vodka plus the bottle)

½ long red chilli, chopped

1 lemongrass stalk, cut into short pieces

1 teaspoon dark soy sauce

2 teaspoons black peppercorns

a slice of fresh horseradish, peeled

75ml dry sherry

To serve:

tomato juice, well chilled

slices of lemon

ice cubes

celery sticks

1 First clean the mushrooms by wiping them with damp kitchen paper. Cut them lengthways into quarters.

2 Empty the vodka into a jug. Put the cleaned mushrooms, chilli, lemongrass, soy sauce, peppercorns and horseradish into the vodka bottle. Add the sherry and pour 425ml vodka back into the bottle. Screw on the top and leave to infuse for at least 1 month.

3 Serve in small glasses with tomato juice, adding a slice of lemon, ice cubes and a celery stick to each glass.

WILD MUSHROOM SPRING ROLLS

This makes an interesting alternative to traditional spring rolls. Serve as an accompaniment or as part of a vegetarian meal.

Serves 4

2 tablespoons olive oil

1 shallot, finely chopped

1cm piece of fresh ginger, finely chopped

2 garlic cloves, finely chopped

250g mixed wild mushrooms, very finely chopped

10 large basil leaves, chopped

6 sheets of filo pastry

100g unsalted butter, melted

sea salt and black pepper

1 Heat the oil in a frying pan, add the shallot and cook gently until softened. Add the ginger and garlic, then the mushrooms, and cook over a low heat for 5 minutes, until the mushrooms are tender. Add the basil, season well with salt and pepper and leave to cool.

2 Lay a sheet of filo pastry on a work surface, brush it with melted butter and place another sheet on top. Cut into 4 squares. Put a tablespoon of the mushroom mixture in the corner of a filo square, fold in the sides and then roll up. Put on to a baking sheet. Repeat with the remaining filo squares, then with the remaining sheets of filo and mushroom mixture to make 12 rolls in total.

3 Brush the spring rolls with melted butter. Place in an oven preheated to 190°C/Gas Mark 5 and bake for about 15 minutes or until golden brown.

A galantine is rather an old-fashioned dish but wonderful nevertheless: a boned-out chicken is stuffed, simmered very slowly in water and then served cold. It's an impressive addition to a buffet, and although there's quite a lot of work involved you can do the whole thing in advance.

GALANTINE OF CHICKEN

stuffed with chorizo

To bone the chicken, follow steps 1 to 11

SERVES 6–8

1 medium chicken

30g unsalted butter

50g onion, finely chopped

2 tablespoons finely diced celery

75g button mushrooms, thinly sliced

200g chorizo, cut into slices 1cm thick

250g belly pork, finely minced

2 tablespoons finely chopped parsley

1 tablespoon roughly chopped tarragon

1 egg

sea salt and black pepper

FOR THE WALNUT, CHICORY AND ORANGE SALAD:

2 heads of chicory

200g wild rocket

200g watercress

40 walnut halves

2 oranges

200ml extra virgin olive oil

100ml walnut oil

juice of 1 orange

1 teaspoon caster sugar

fine sea salt and black pepper

1 To bone the chicken, first remove the wishbone. Lift up the skin, then run around the outside of the bone with the point of a sharp knife.

2 Nick the sinew at the top and pull the wishbone out.

3 Lay the chicken, breast-side down, on the chopping board and cut through the skin along the backbone down to the bone.

4 Carefully loosen the skin. Working on one side, separate the flesh from the bone, following the line of the carcass with the knife.

5 To enable you to do this all the way along, cut through the shoulder joint and thigh joint so they lie flat.

6 Keep working down until the breast is removed. Repeat on the other side.

7 Cut the carcass off and remove.

8 Cut the sinews around the thigh bone, then gently scrape the flesh from the bone. Cut off the bone at the joint with the drumstick. Leave the drumstick in and the knuckle on.

9 Cut around the shoulder bone, then gently scrape the flesh from the bone and cut out the bone.

10 Cut off the wings and discard, or keep to make stock.

11 Lay the carcass out flat, skin-side down, on the chopping board, then cut around the parson's nose and remove.

12 To make the stuffing, melt the butter in a small frying pan, add the onion and celery and cook until softened.

13 Add the mushrooms and cook for 3 minutes or until very soft. Drain and leave to cool.

14 Heat a dry frying pan, add the chorizo and cook for a few minutes, until the fat runs out.

15 Remove from the pan, drain on kitchen paper and leave to cool. Cut each piece of chorizo into quarters.

16 Put the chorizo into a large bowl with the minced pork, then add the herbs, egg and the onion mixture. Season well and mix thoroughly.

17 Season the boned chicken (still laying skin-side down) with salt and pepper. Arrange the stuffing down the centre and pat to form a firm mound.

18 Bring the sides of the chicken up and then the flap at the wishbone end.

19 Using a butchery needle threaded with butcher's string, sew up the chicken as tightly as possible and then tie the ends of the string together.

20 Using more butcher's string, tie the drumsticks together.

21 Wrap the chicken up in muslin and tie securely with string.

22 Put the chicken into a large saucepan of barely simmering water and cook gently for 1½ hours.

23 Remove the pan from the heat, carefully lift out the chicken and put it on to a dish. Cut off any excess muslin, but leave the chicken wrapped up.

24 Wrap the hot chicken in cling film, rolling it tightly around the bird a few times to seal in the juices. Leave the chicken to cool for at least 12 hours at room temperature.

25 To make the salad, cut the root from the chicory, then separate the leaves and slice them lengthways on the diagonal.

26 Put the chicory leaves into a large bowl with the rocket, watercress and walnuts.

27 Cut the peel and all the white pith from the oranges. Cut between the membranes to remove the segments and set them aside.

28 Put both oils, the orange juice and sugar into a bowl, season with salt and pepper and whisk together.

29 Pour the dressing over the salad and toss. Scatter the orange segments on the top.

30 Remove the cling film and muslin from the galantine of chicken and pull out the string Cut into slices and serve with the salad.

TIPS AND IDEAS

■ This boning technique works for other birds too, such as duck, guinea fowl and pheasant.

■ Do try to buy a free-range, preferably organic, chicken. Not only will the bird have led a better life but the flavour and texture will also be well worth the extra cost.

■ Don't throw away the chicken bones and wings; instead, use them to make stock. If you don't want to use them straight away, they will keep well in the freezer.

■ It's worth investing in a proper boning knife – a short, sturdy knife with a blade that tapers in.

■ Make friends with your butcher and ask for some butcher's string for sewing up the bird – it's the best thing for the job.

■ If you don't have a butchery needle, you could use a large tapestry needle instead.

■ If you really don't want to sew up the bird, you can wrap it in cling film to secure it tightly.

■ When you cook the chicken, make sure the water is barely simmering, to ensure the meat is tender.

■ Wrapping the bird in cling film after cooking helps it retain all the juices, so it stays moist.

■ At the end of step 24, you could unwrap the cooled chicken, discarding the muslin, then wrap it tightly in fresh cling film before storing in the fridge. Slice the galantine with the cling film on, remembering to remove it from each slice before serving – this ensures the galantine doesn't fall apart when slicing.

■ The galantine will keep well in the fridge for several days.

galantine of chicken variations

Galantine of Chicken with Nut Stuffing – follow the recipe on pages 38–41, omitting the fried chorizo from the stuffing and add a handful of pistachios, hazelnuts or walnuts to the mixture instead.

Galantine of Chicken with Wild Mushroom Stuffing – follow the recipe on pages 38–41, omitting the fried chorizo from the stuffing. Replace the button mushrooms with wild mushrooms and increase the quantity to 250g.

Galantine of Chicken with Black Pudding Stuffing – follow the recipe on pages 38–41, replacing the chorizo with black pudding.

Galantine of Chicken with Herb Stuffing – follow the recipe on pages 38–41, omitting the fried chorizo and add plenty of chopped herbs to the pork mixture.

Galantine of Pheasant – follow the recipe on pages 38–41, using a pheasant instead of a chicken and reducing the cooking time to 1 hour 10 minutes.

Galantine of Poussin – follow the recipe on pages 38–41, using a poussin instead of a chicken and reducing the cooking time to 1 hour.

Galantine of Quail – follow the recipe on pages 38–41, using quails instead of chicken and cook them for 45 minutes. See page 87 for details of boning quail.

CHICKEN WITH FRENCH BEANS IN A PAPER BAG

Serves 4

4 small chicken breasts, skinned and boned

2 tablespoons olive oil

200ml chicken stock

200g fine French beans, topped and tailed

8 spring onions, finely chopped

2 garlic cloves, finely chopped

1cm piece of fresh ginger, finely chopped

¼ red chilli, finely chopped

1 tablespoon oyster sauce

sea salt and black pepper

1 Season the chicken breasts with salt and pepper. Heat 1 tablespoon of the oil in a frying pan, add the chicken and cook over a medium heat for 2 minutes on each side. Transfer to a plate. Add the stock to the pan and simmer until reduced by half. Pour into a jug and reserve.

2 Meanwhile, cook the beans in boiling salted water for 3–4 minutes, until just tender, then drain.

3 Wipe out the frying pan, heat the remaining oil in it and add half the spring onions, plus the garlic, ginger and chilli. Cook for 1–2 minutes. Toss in the beans and mix well. Add the oyster sauce, season with salt and pepper and remove from the heat.

4 Take 4 large pieces of greaseproof paper. Fold each piece in half, then divide the bean mixture between them, piling it on the centre of one half. Cut each breast into thirds and place on top of the beans, then add the remaining spring onions. Pour a little of the reserved stock over each pile of ingredients. Bring the other half of the paper over the filling and crimp the edges together to seal. Slide the paper parcels on to a baking sheet, place in an oven preheated to 190°C/ Gas Mark 5 and cook for 15 minutes.

5 Transfer each parcel directly to a serving plate and open to serve, or slide the contents on to the plate. Serve with Wild Mushroom Spring Rolls (see page 31).

CHICKEN LEGS STUFFED WITH MUSHROOMS

A sophisticated way of serving a relatively economical cut, this uses chicken legs to their best advantage. I find them so much tastier than the breast.

Serves 4

4 chicken legs

25g unsalted butter

75g button mushrooms, sliced

1 tablespoon chopped thyme

150g chicken thigh meat

1 egg white

100ml double cream

50g pistachio nuts, chopped

2 tablespoons olive oil

sea salt and black pepper

1 To bone the chicken legs, put them skin-side down on a board and run a knife along the bone to cut the skin. Carefully scrape the meat away from the bone with the knife, then cut the bone away from the skin to release it. Cut out any sinews from the leg.

2 Melt the butter in a small frying pan, add the mushrooms and cook gently for 5 minutes. Add the thyme and season well with salt and pepper. Leave to cool.

3 Put the chicken thigh meat into a food processor and process roughly, then add the egg white and process again until combined. Mix in the cream in a slow, steady stream using the pulse button, but be careful not to over-process, otherwise the cream will curdle. Transfer to a bowl and season well with salt and pepper. Fold in the cooled mushroom mixture and pistachio nuts.

4 Lay the boned legs out, skin-side down, on a board. Season with salt and pepper. Divide the filling mixture between the legs, and arranging it in a roll in the centre of the thigh. Position a roll of cling film behind the board, then pull the sheet of film forward. Place a leg on the cling film and roll up a few times to make a tightly sealed package. Repeat with the remaining legs.

5 Place the chicken rolls in a steamer and steam for 15 minutes. Remove from the steamer and leave to cool completely, then unwrap the cling film. (You can prepare them up to this stage a day in advance.)

6 When ready to serve, heat the oil in a frying pan over a high heat, add the chicken legs and sear until coloured on all sides. Transfer to a roasting tray and place in an oven preheated to 200°C/Gas Mark 6 for 10 minutes to heat through. Remove from the oven and leave to rest for 10 minutes before cutting. They are very good served with a plain risotto or a salad.

CHICKEN KIEV

I absolutely love this dish. Just make sure the chicken breasts are not too big, so they will cook in the time given below — you can't stick a knife in to check whether they are done or all the delicious garlic butter will ooze out.

Serves 4

125g soft unsalted butter

2 large garlic cloves, finely chopped

2 tablespoons finely chopped parsley

juice and grated zest of 1 lemon

4 medium chicken breasts, skinned and boned

sunflower oil for deep-frying

sea salt and black pepper

For the coating:

150g plain flour, seasoned well with sea salt and black pepper

4 eggs, beaten

300g fresh fine white breadcrumbs

Chicken Kiev variation

Herbed Chicken Breasts – make the filling as above using 125g soft unsalted butter, 1 finely chopped garlic clove and 2 tablespoons finely chopped flat-leaf parsley, seasoning well with salt and pepper. Fill the chicken breasts as above. Mix together 4 rounded tablespoons chopped flat-leaf parsley and 1 rounded tablespoon each of chopped tarragon and finely chopped thyme in a shallow bowl. Season with salt and pepper. Brush each chicken breast with 30g melted unsalted butter, then dip into the herb mixture. Heat 2 tablespoons olive oil in a large frying pan, add the chicken breasts and cook for about 2 minutes on each side. Transfer to a baking tray, place in an oven preheated to 180°C/Gas Mark 4 and cook for a further 20 minutes, until golden.

1 For the filling, put the butter, garlic and parsley into a bowl and mix well. Gradually beat in the lemon juice and zest. Divide the butter into 4 neat portions, place on a plate and cover with cling film. Leave in the fridge for 30 minutes.

2 Meanwhile, put the chicken breasts on a chopping board and level them out by gently bashing them with the base of a heavy pan – but don't overdo it and make them thin.

3 Remove the butter mixture from the fridge. Cut a horizontal slit in each chicken breast and, with your fingers or the knife, work it into a pocket large enough to hold the filling mixture, being careful not to tear holes in the chicken. Season the flesh inside with salt and pepper, then push the butter right in, leaving a rim of chicken to seal. Cover the chicken and leave in the fridge for 1 hour.

4 To coat the chicken, put the seasoned flour into a shallow bowl, the beaten eggs into a separate bowl and the breadcrumbs into another bowl. Brush the inside edges of the pocket of each breast with beaten egg and press together to seal. Turn each breast in the flour, brush off any excess, then dip into the beaten eggs and finally roll in the breadcrumbs to coat. Repeat the process so that they each have a double coating.

5 Heat some sunflower oil to 160°C in a deep-fat fryer or a large, deep saucepan. Fry the chicken for about 10–12 minutes or until golden brown. Drain on kitchen paper. Alternatively, place the chicken on a baking tray in an oven preheated to 180°C/Gas Mark 4 and cook for 25 minutes, until golden brown. Serve straight away, with a herb salad.

CHICKEN, LEEK AND MUSHROOM PIE

This chicken pie is a wonderful dish for a family gathering.

Serves 6–8

2 large chicken legs, boned (see page 44) and skinned

4 chicken breasts, skinned and boned

250g button mushrooms

900ml chicken stock

60g unsalted butter, plus extra for greasing

3 tablespoons olive oil

1 onion, finely diced

2 large leeks, white part only, thinly sliced

2 garlic cloves, finely chopped

2 celery sticks, finely chopped

1½ tablespoons dried tarragon

300g back bacon, cut into batons

40g plain flour, plus extra for dusting

150ml white wine

200ml double cream

450g puff pastry

1 egg, beaten, to glaze

sea salt and black pepper

1 Cut the chicken into 2.5cm pieces and set aside.

2 Put the mushrooms into a large frying pan, add 400ml of the stock, bring to the boil and simmer for 15 minutes. Strain and reserve the mushrooms and cooking liquid separately.

3 Wipe out the frying pan. Melt the butter in it with 1 tablespoon of the olive oil, add the chicken pieces and cook until lightly browned on all sides; do this in batches so as not to overcrowd the pan. Remove from the pan and transfer to a large saucepan. Add the remaining 2 tablespoons oil to the frying pan, then add the onion, leeks, garlic, celery and tarragon. Cook gently until soft but not browned. Transfer to the saucepan. Add the bacon batons to the frying pan and fry until browned, then transfer to the saucepan. Add the flour to the saucepan and mix well.

4 Add the wine to the frying pan and bring to a simmer, stirring and scraping the base of the pan to deglaze it. Pour into the saucepan. Add enough of the remaining stock to cover, season with salt and pepper and mix well. Cover the pan and cook over a low heat for 35 minutes.

5 Using a slotted spoon, transfer all the ingredients from the saucepan to a 1.5–2 litre pie dish. Boil the liquid left in the pan until reduced by half, then add the cream, whisking gently with a balloon whisk. Adjust the seasoning and cook for a further 5 minutes. Pour enough of this sauce into the pie dish to just cover all the ingredients, reserving any excess to serve with the pie. Leave to cool.

6 Roll out the puff pastry on a lightly floured work surface until slightly larger than the dish. Grease the dish edges well, then cut narrow strips of pastry to fit the edges. Place on the dish and brush with a little beaten egg. Cover the dish with the remaining pastry and press the edges together to seal. Make a hole in the centre of the pastry and brush all over with the beaten egg.

7 Place in an oven preheated to 180°C/Gas Mark 4 and bake for 25 minutes. Turn the oven down to 150°C/Gas Mark 2 and cook for a further 20–25 minutes, until golden brown, being careful not to burn the pastry.

BALLOTINE OF DUCK WITH PHEASANT

Here, a whole duck is boned, filled with a wild mushroom stuffing and a boned-out pheasant and then roasted. You could change the flavours of the stuffing to your liking.

Serves 8

1 large duck, boned (see page 39)

1 pheasant, boned (see page 39), skinned and drumsticks removed (use for another recipe or for making stock)

1 large Spanish onion, chopped

2 carrots, peeled and chopped

1 teaspoon coarse sea salt

sea salt and black pepper

For the stuffing:

60g unsalted butter

1 onion, finely chopped

1 garlic clove, finely chopped

100g mixed wild mushrooms, finely chopped

1 teaspoon chopped thyme

1 teaspoon dried rosemary

50ml cognac (optional)

1 duck liver, chopped

350g belly pork, finely minced

1 Make the stuffing. Melt the butter in a frying pan, add the onion and garlic and cook gently until softened. Add the wild mushrooms, thyme and rosemary and cook for 2–3 minutes longer. Pour over the cognac, if using, and then with great care ignite it with a long match or by angling the far side of the pan towards the gas flame to flambé. When the flames have died down, add the duck liver and cook for a few seconds, stirring, until cooked but still pink in the centre. Leave to cool.

2 Put the minced pork into a large bowl, add the duck liver and wild mushroom mixture and season well with salt and pepper. Mix together well.

3 Lay the duck, skin-side down, on a work surface and season with salt and pepper. Spread half of the stuffing down the centre. Lay the pheasant meat on top and spread the remaining stuffing over the pheasant. Bring the sides of the duck up and then the skin at the wishbone end. Using a butchery needle or large tapestry needle threaded with butcher's string, sew up as tightly as possible. Leave a long length of string on one end and then, using another length of string on the other end, tie the lengths together but not too tightly. Tie the drumsticks together so that it looks like a duck again (see page 40, steps 18–20). Tie 3 pieces of string around the whole duck, not too tightly but enough to hold it in place and give it a little more stability.

4 Put the onion and carrots into a large roasting tin, then lay the duck on top. Sprinkle with the coarse sea salt and place in an oven preheated to 180°C/Gas Mark 4. Cook for 1½ hours, then turn the oven down to 160°C/Gas Mark 3 and cook for a further 20 minutes. Remove from the oven, transfer to a warm plate and leave to rest for 25 minutes before carving.

5 Pull the string out of the duck and cut the ballotine into slices, then serve with roasted root vegetables.

POACHED BREAST OF DUCK WITH VEGETABLE FRICASSÉE

It's nice to poach meat occasionally. It's such a healthy cooking method and retains the pure flavour of the meat. The trick with poaching is to make sure the liquid is barely simmering — there should be just a few bubbles breaking the surface. If it simmers too vigorously, the meat will be tough.

Serves 2

2 medium duck breasts, skinned

1 litre well-flavoured chicken stock

30g unsalted butter

sea salt and black pepper

sprigs of chervil and tarragon, to garnish

For the vegetables:

500ml chicken stock

6 baby carrots, left whole, or larger carrots cut into batons

1 courgette, cut into batons

20 fine French beans, topped and tailed

6 baby onions, peeled but left whole, or baby leeks

100g small mushrooms

6 asparagus spears, trimmed

2 tablespoons finely chopped parsley

For the white sauce:

15g unsalted butter

15g plain flour

100ml double cream

2–3 tablespoons grated Fountains Gold or Cheddar cheese

1 Remove all sinews from the duck breasts. Cover the duck and leave in the fridge until required.

2 To prepare the vegetables, bring 300ml of the stock to the boil in a saucepan. Add the carrots and cook for 1 minute, then remove with a slotted spoon and set aside. Add the courgette and cook for 1 minute, then remove with a slotted spoon, refresh under cold running water and drain. Repeat with the French beans. Pour the stock left in the pan into a jug – you should have about 200ml. Reserve for the sauce.

3 Heat the remaining 200ml stock in the saucepan. Add the onions or leeks and cook for 3 minutes, then remove with a slotted spoon. Add the mushrooms and cook for 4 minutes, then drain. Discard the stock. Cook the asparagus in a saucepan of boiling salted water for 1 minute, then drain well.

4 To make the sauce, melt the butter in a small saucepan. Add the flour and cook, stirring, over a low heat for 1 minute. Gradually add the reserved stock from cooking the vegetables, stirring constantly with a wooden spoon until smooth, then stir in the cream. Bring to the boil and simmer over a low heat for 2 minutes. Stir in the cheese and season well with salt and pepper. You can prepare the dish up to this stage in advance.

5 When you are ready to serve, bring the 1 litre stock to a simmer in a saucepan. Add the duck breasts and poach over a very low heat for 8 minutes. Remove from the pan, season and leave to rest for 5 minutes.

6 Gently reheat half the vegetables in the sauce. Melt the butter in a frying pan, add the remaining vegetables and toss over a medium heat until thoroughly hot. Season well with salt and pepper.

7 Put a spoonful of vegetables in sauce in the centre of each of 2 large serving bowls, then top with the other vegetables. Slice each duck breast into 5 pieces and arrange on top. Garnish with sprigs of chervil and tarragon.

DUCK PÂTÉ

This is a splendid rustic pâté for an informal meal. It will keep in the fridge for about 4 days.

Serves 8

2 large duck breasts, skinned

500g pork shoulder, minced

100g chicken livers

30g unsalted butter, plus extra for greasing

2 garlic cloves, finely chopped

50g fresh white breadcrumbs

100ml milk

1 egg

2 tablespoons finely chopped parsley

1 tablespoon thyme leaves

1 teaspoon freshly grated nutmeg

sea salt and black pepper

1 Remove all sinews from the duck breasts. Put the meat into a food processor and process until finely minced but still with some texture. Add to the minced pork in a bowl.

2 Clean the chicken livers by removing the veins. Melt the butter in a frying pan, add the livers and cook over a fairly high heat until browned on the outside but still pink inside. Remove from the pan, chop finely and leave to cool.

3 Add the chicken livers to the pork with the garlic. Mix the breadcrumbs with the milk, then add to the pork with all the remaining ingredients. Season well with salt and pepper.

4 Grease a large soufflé dish or a small casserole dish. Fill with the mixture and cover with foil. Stand the dish in a roasting tin and pour enough cold water into the tin to come halfway up the side of the dish. Place in an oven preheated to 180°C/Gas Mark 4 and cook for 20 minutes. Turn the oven down to 140°C/Gas Mark 1 and cook for a further hour. Remove from the oven and leave to cool. Serve with bread and chutney.

DUCK BREASTS WITH BLACKCURRANT SAUCE

This is such a simple way of serving duck breasts, and if you keep blackcurrants in the freezer it can be made at any time of year. The tartness of the blackcurrants cuts the fatty richness of the duck.

Serves 4

200g fresh or frozen blackcurrants

4 duck breasts, skin on

60g unsalted butter

25g streaky bacon, diced

50g onion, finely chopped

150ml port

250ml well-flavoured chicken stock

sea salt and black pepper

1 Purée the blackcurrants in a blender. Pass through a fine sieve and reserve.

2 Cut about 7 slashes in the skin of each duck breast, being careful not to cut into the flesh. Heat a dry frying pan over a low–medium heat, sprinkle some salt into the pan, then add the duck breasts, skin-side down, and press them down with a spatula or fish slice. Cook for 6 minutes without moving them. Turn them over and cook for a further 5 minutes. Remove from the pan and leave to rest for 10 minutes.

3 To make the sauce, melt 30g of the butter in a saucepan, add the bacon and onion and cook until the bacon is browned and the onion is soft. Add the port and boil until reduced by half. Add the stock and boil until reduced by half again. Stir in the blackcurrant purée and cook until thickened to a sauce consistency. Season well with salt and pepper.

4 Pass the sauce through a fine sieve into a small saucepan. Bring to a simmer, then add the remaining 30g butter, diced, a few pieces at a time, whisking constantly with a balloon whisk. Serve with the duck breasts.

PEKING DUCK WITH PANCAKES

I've been making this recipe for years and my family loves it. It's essential to hang the duck to get rid of the moisture, so the skin rises up and becomes really crisp during cooking. I hang it in my garage, but if you don't have a suitable outbuilding, just leave it in the coolest part of your house. The pancakes are a lot of fun to make. Be sure to oil them really well so they don't stick together.

Serves 6

1 medium duck

2 tablespoons honey, dissolved in
2 tablespoons water

2 tablespoons dark soy sauce

For the pancakes:

500g plain flour

½ teaspoon chilli powder (optional)

1 teaspoon fine sea salt

400ml water

50ml vegetable oil

To serve:

150ml hoisin sauce

2 bunches of spring onions, cut into fine strips
and then into 3cm lengths

1 cucumber, cut into fine strips

1 Rinse the duck, drain and then remove any fat from the cavity opening and around the neck. Plunge the duck into a large saucepan of boiling water and cook for 1 minute to tighten the skin. Remove and drain, then dry thoroughly.

2 While the skin is still warm, mix the diluted honey and soy sauce together and brush all over the duck. Hang the duck up to dry in a cool, airy place for at least 12 hours or overnight. Brush occasionally with the remaining honey mixture.

3 Set the duck on a rack in a roasting tin. Place in an oven preheated to 200°C/Gas Mark 6 and roast for 1½ hours without basting or turning. Check to make sure that the duck is not over-browning, and if it is, cover it loosely with foil.

4 Meanwhile, make the pancakes. Put the flour, chilli powder, if using, and salt into a large bowl. Bring the water to the boil and slowly add to the flour mixture, stirring constantly. Add 2 teaspoons of the oil and mix to a smooth dough. Divide the dough in half. Roll each half into a sausage shape and cut into 12 pieces. Form a piece of dough into a ball, then push down and roll out into a small circle. Repeat with another ball of dough. Brush a little of the oil all over one of the circles of dough right to the edge, then place the other circle of dough on top. Roll into a pancake about 18–20cm round. Repeat with the remaining dough to make 12 pancakes.

5 Heat a dry, non-stick frying pan until medium hot, add one double pancake and cook over a low heat for at least 2 minutes on each side, until dry to the touch. Remove from the pan, peel the 2 pancakes apart and set aside. Repeat with the remaining pancakes. When ready to serve, heat the pancakes in a steamer or wrap in foil and heat up in the oven.

6 Remove the cooked duck from the oven. Take off the skin and cut into small slices, then carve the meat, or carve both the skin and meat together. Arrange on a serving plate.

7 To eat, spread a little hoisin sauce over a pancake, add a few strips of spring onion and cucumber, then some duck skin and meat and roll up the pancake. Turn up the bottom edge to prevent the contents from falling out.

DUCK BREASTS WITH LENTIL SALAD AND KIWI DRESSING

In general, I am not a fan of kiwi fruit but I do enjoy them puréed in this refreshing, slightly bitter-sweet dressing. We grow tiny ones against the wall at Swinton Park and they are very successful. The dressing doesn't keep well, so do use it on the day you make it.

Serves 4

4 duck breasts, skin on

4 tablespoons dark soy sauce

4 tablespoons soft brown sugar

2 tablespoons runny honey

2 teaspoons English mustard powder

25g unsalted butter

1 frisée lettuce

sea salt and black pepper

micro herbs or small salad leaves, to garnish

For the lentil salad:

1 tablespoon olive oil

25g onion, finely chopped

75g smoked streaky bacon, finely chopped

1 garlic clove, chopped

75g Puy lentils

350ml chicken stock, plus a little extra if needed

1 tablespoon thyme leaves

1 bay leaf

For the kiwi dressing:

2 kiwi fruit, peeled and chopped

½ small green chilli, finely chopped

juice and grated zest of ½ lemon

4 mint leaves, chopped

1 teaspoon white wine vinegar

75ml extra virgin olive oil

1 Cook the lentils. Heat the oil in a saucepan, add the onion with the bacon and garlic and cook until softened. Add the lentils, stock, thyme and bay leaf. Bring to the boil, then reduce the heat and simmer for about 20–25 minutes, until the lentils are tender – you may need to add more stock if they become too dry. Leave to cool and season well with salt and pepper.

2 For the dressing, put the kiwi fruit, chilli, lemon juice and zest, mint and vinegar into a blender. Blend while adding the oil in a slow, steady stream. Season with salt and pepper.

3 Cut about 7 slashes in the skin of each duck breast, taking care not to cut into the flesh. Heat a dry frying pan over a low–medium heat, sprinkle some salt into the pan, then add the duck breasts, skin-side down, and press them down with a spatula or fish slice. Cook without moving them for 5 minutes or until the skin is dark brown. Transfer to a plate. Wipe the pan clean.

4 Mix the soy sauce, sugar, honey and mustard together in a small saucepan, bring to the boil and simmer until reduced by almost a third.

5 Melt the butter in the cleaned frying pan over a medium heat. Add the duck breasts, skin-side up, and cook for 1 minute. Add the reduced soy and honey mixture and cook the duck for a further 4 minutes, basting constantly – be careful not to burn. The duck should be nice and sticky, so cook to reduce the sauce a little further if necessary. Remove from the pan and leave to rest.

6 While the duck is resting, wash the frisée, discarding any yellow leaves, drain well and shake dry in a clean tea towel. Put the frisée into a large bowl and mix in the lentils with 2 teaspoons of the dressing. Season with salt and pepper.

7 To serve, divide the frisée and lentil salad between serving plates. Slice the duck breasts, place on top and spoon some dressing around. Garnish with micro herbs or small salad leaves.

I do enjoy Thai curries. A chicken curry made with a whole, jointed chicken will give the best flavour.

THAI CHICKEN CURRY

with cashew nuts

To joint the chicken, follow steps 1 to 9

SERVES 4

1 medium chicken

100ml rapeseed oil

1 Spanish onion, thinly sliced

2 green chillies, thinly sliced

1 garlic clove, crushed

150ml chicken stock

450ml coconut milk

grated zest of ½ lemon

3 kaffir lime leaves

120g salted cashew nuts

a handful of coriander leaves

sea salt and black pepper

FOR THE SPICE POWDER:

2 tablespoons coriander seeds

1 tablespoon cumin seeds

1 teaspoon white peppercorns

seeds from 20 green cardamom pods

2 cloves

3 teaspoons turmeric

1 teaspoon freshly grated nutmeg

1 teaspoon dried chilli powder

FOR THE FRAGRANT RICE:

350g basmati rice

½ teaspoon caraway seeds

4 cloves

6 green cardamom pods

2 bay leaves

about 450ml chicken stock

a pinch of sea salt

1 To remove the wishbone, lift up the skin, then run around the outside of the bone with the point of a sharp knife.

2 Nick the sinew at the top and pull the wishbone out.

3 Loosen one leg and thigh by cutting through the skin at the top of the leg, against the carcass.

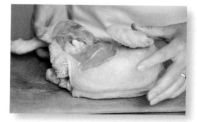

4 Then snap the leg out of its socket, twisting it to break the joint, and cut through the flesh to remove the leg. Repeat on the other side of the bird.

5 To remove one breast and wing, cut down through the carcass, keeping the knife close to the bone as you scrape away the flesh, making sure that the wing is attached to the breast.

6 Repeat on the other side to remove the second breast and wing. Cut off the wing tips and discard.

7 Now divide the 4 joints into 8. Place each leg skin-side down and feel with your thumb for the joint. Cut through the joint.

8 Then neaten the drumsticks by cutting off the knuckle.

9 Cut each breast in half on the diagonal, leaving about one-third attached to the wing.

10 To prepare the spice powder, heat a dry frying pan, then add all the whole spices.

11 Cook over a medium heat for a few minutes until they become aromatic, stirring often. Remove from the pan and leave to cool.

12 Put into a mortar and grind with a pestle as finely as possible, or use an electric grinder. Mix with the remaining spices.

13 Mix 1 tablespoon of the spice powder with 2 tablespoons of the rapeseed oil (store the remaining spice powder in an airtight jar).

14 Rub the spice mixture into the chicken pieces. Season with salt.

15 Heat the remaining oil in a sauté pan, add the onion and cook for 3 minutes, until softened. Remove from the pan.

16 Add the chicken and cook until browned on all sides.

17 Return the onion to the pan and add the chillies and garlic. Pour in the stock and coconut milk and add the lemon zest and lime leaves.

18 Bring to a simmer and cook for 15 minutes. Add the cashew nuts and cook for a further 10 minutes, until the chicken is tender.

19 Meanwhile, prepare the rice. Tip it into a sieve and rinse under cold running water, then drain well.

20 Put the caraway seeds, cloves, cardamom pods and bay leaves into a square of muslin, gather the sides together and tie with a piece of string.

21 Put the rice into a large saucepan, pour in the stock to come 1cm above the rice and add the salt. Add the spice parcel to the pan.

22 Bring to the boil, then cover the pan, reduce the heat to as low as possible and simmer for 10 minutes.

23 Turn off the heat and leave with the lid on for a further 10 minutes to allow the spices to infuse. Remove the spice parcel, then fluff the rice up gently with a fork.

24 Toss the coriander leaves into the curry and serve with the rice.

Thai chicken curry variations

Thai Chicken Curry with Peanuts – follow the recipe on pages 54–56, replacing the cashew nuts with salted peanuts. Hazelnuts would also be very good.

Thai Fish Curry – follow the recipe on pages 54–56, replacing the chicken with 650g white fish fillets, skinned and cut into chunks. Brown the fish as for the chicken, then remove it from the pan and set aside while you continue with the curry. Return the fish to the pan 5 minutes before the end.

Thai Prawn Curry – follow the recipe on pages 54–56, replacing the chicken with 500g peeled raw prawns, adding them about 5 minutes before the end.

Thai Chicken and Mango Curry – follow the recipe on pages 54–56, adding 1 peeled, stoned and diced mango with the cashew nuts.

Thai Lamb Curry – follow the recipe on pages 54–56, replacing the chicken with 600g loin of lamb, cut into 2.5cm cubes. Brown it really well so it caramelises.

TIPS AND IDEAS

■ Other birds, such as game birds, duck and guinea fowl, can be jointed in exactly the same way.

■ The reason for removing the wishbone before jointing the chicken is so you keep all the breast. This is particularly important when jointing duck, as otherwise you can end up leaving a lot of the breast on the carcass.

■ A boning knife will give you the best results when jointing poultry.

■ If you want bigger portions, leave the legs and breasts whole rather than cutting them in half.

■ It is best to cook curries for the shortest possible time, so the flavours stay fresh and vibrant.

■ It's well worth making your own spice powders as the flavours are more vibrant than the ones you buy.

■ Toasting the spices briefly in a dry frying pan enhances their flavour and they give off a marvellous aroma.

■ I grind spices in an electric coffee grinder. It's less work than a mortar and pestle (though not as much fun!).

■ Dried kaffir lime leaves are readily available, fresh ones more difficult to find. I have recently discovered that the dried leaves make a wonderfully refreshing tea – simply pour boiling water over them and leave to infuse.

■ Don't cook the rice in too much liquid or it will be waterlogged and soggy. My grandmother taught me the secret of cooking rice: add just enough liquid to come a thumbnail's depth above it. In this way, the rice absorbs it all so the end result is dry and fluffy.

■ In this recipe the rice is cooked in stock for extra flavour but you can, of course, use water for plain boiled rice.

■ Adding the spices to the rice in a bag and then removing them gives a gentler flavour. You could also heat the stock with the spice bag beforehand to infuse it, if you prefer.

BARBECUE CHICKEN THIGHS

These are coated in a lovely marinade that works well with other meats, such as pork. Although the instructions below are for cooking in the oven, you could easily cook the chicken thighs on a barbecue in summer.

Serves 4

8 chicken thighs, skin on

sprigs of flat-leaf parsley, to garnish

For the barbecue marinade:

125g hoisin sauce

75g tomato ketchup

2 tablespoons runny honey

2 tablespoons sweet chilli sauce

1 rounded teaspoon ground cumin

2 tablespoons soy sauce

2 tablespoons finely grated fresh ginger (optional)

2 garlic cloves, finely grated

juice of 2 limes

1 teaspoon chilli powder

1 Mix all the ingredients for the marinade together in a bowl.

2 Dip each thigh into the marinade and then put into a roasting tray. If you have time, cover and leave to marinate in the fridge for a few hours or overnight.

3 When ready to cook, place in an oven preheated to 180°C/Gas Mark 4 and bake for 45 minutes or until cooked through, turning over halfway through cooking. To test for doneness, insert a knife into the thickest part of the meat, near the bone – if the juices run clear, the chicken is done.

4 Remove from the oven and serve garnished with sprigs of flat-leaf parsley.

CHICKEN FRICASSÉE

Serves 4

30g unsalted butter

1 tablespoon olive oil

1 medium chicken, cut into 8 portions (see page 55)

150ml white wine

1 bouquet garni

800ml chicken stock

20 small shallots

150g button mushrooms

150ml double cream

Beurre Manié (see page 70, tips), made with 15g soft unsalted butter and 15g plain flour (optional)

sea salt and black pepper

2 tablespoons finely chopped parsley, to garnish

1 Melt the butter with the oil in a large saucepan. Season the chicken, add to the pan and cook over a medium heat until browned on all sides. Add the wine and cook for a couple of minutes, until reduced by about a third. Add the bouquet garni and enough of the stock to come level with the top of the chicken and simmer for 20 minutes, until the chicken is cooked through.

2 Meanwhile, peel the shallots and carefully cut the tops off, but don't remove the root. Bring the remaining stock to a simmer in a saucepan, add the shallots and cook for 5 minutes or until soft. Remove from the pan. Add the mushrooms and cook for 5 minutes, then drain well.

3 Remove the cooked chicken from the pan and set aside. Simmer the sauce until reduced by half, then stir in the cream and simmer for 3–4 minutes. Whisk in the *beurre manié* a small piece at a time if the sauce needs thickening. Season well with salt and pepper. Return the chicken to the sauce with the shallots and mushrooms and heat through. Sprinkle with the parsley to garnish. Serve with rice.

CHICKEN TAGINE

This contains all the lovely, fragrant flavours of North Africa. Preserved lemons add a unique taste and are available from many delis and large supermarkets.

Serves 4

1 medium chicken, cut into 8 portions (see page 55)

a drizzle of olive oil

2 onions, chopped

10 Hunza apricots, stoned and cut in half

about 1 litre chicken stock

4 small preserved lemons

1 teaspoon granulated sugar

juice of 1 lemon

2 tablespoons chopped flat-leaf parsley

2 tablespoons chopped coriander

100g green olives, stoned

Beurre Manié (see page 70, tips), made with 15g soft unsalted butter and 15g plain flour (optional)

sea salt and black pepper

For the spicy marinade:

2 garlic cloves, finely chopped

a pinch of saffron strands

1 teaspoon ground cinnamon

1 teaspoon ground ginger

1 teaspoon ground cumin

1 teaspoon paprika

1 teaspoon sea salt

100ml olive oil

1 Prepare the marinade. Mix all the ingredients together in a bowl with some pepper. Spread the mixture over the chicken joints in a dish, cover and leave to marinate in the fridge for several hours or overnight, turning occasionally.

2 Heat the oil in a large frying pan, add the chicken and cook until browned on all sides. Transfer to a large saucepan. Add the onions, apricots and enough stock to come level with the chicken. Bring to the boil, then cover the pan, reduce the heat and simmer for about 25 minutes.

3 Lift out the chicken and apricots and put into a dish. Continue simmering the sauce for about 20 minutes, until it starts to thicken slightly. Meanwhile, cut the preserved lemons into quarters lengthways and remove and discard the flesh, reserving the skin only. Cut into long strips and add to the sauce with the sugar, lemon juice, herbs and olives. Mix together well.

4 Whisk in the *beurre manié* a small piece at a time if the sauce needs thickening slightly. Return the chicken and apricots to the sauce and continue cooking for 15 minutes to combine the flavours. Season with salt and pepper. Serve with couscous or rice.

CHICKEN BREASTS STUFFED WITH MOZZARELLA, SERVED WITH CRISP PANCETTA AND SALAD

I think of this as a light, summery alternative to Chicken Kiev (see page 45). As an alternative to the herb salad, serve with a tomato sauce.

Serves 4

olive oil

1 tablespoon very finely diced shallot

4 small slices of mozzarella cheese

1 teaspoon finely chopped parsley

4 medium chicken breasts, skinned and boned

100g plain flour

2 eggs, beaten

300g fresh fine white breadcrumbs

4 tablespoons sunflower oil

4 rashers of pancetta (or bacon)

sea salt and black pepper

For the salad:

75ml extra virgin olive oil

1 teaspoon white wine vinegar

1 tablespoon finely chopped parsley

2 tomatoes, skinned (see page 278, step 1), deseeded and diced

1 frisée lettuce

a handful of herbs

1 Heat a drizzle of olive oil in a frying pan, add the shallot and cook gently until softened. Put into a bowl, add the mozzarella and parsley and season with salt and pepper. Mix together well.

2 Lay the chicken breasts on a board and level them out by gently bashing them with the base of a heavy pan – don't overdo it and make them thin. Cut a horizontal slit in each chicken breast and gently work into a pocket large enough to hold the mozzarella. Insert a slice of marinated mozzarella into each pocket, leaving a rim of chicken to seal, and season well with salt and pepper.

3 To coat the chicken, put the flour into a shallow bowl, the beaten eggs into a separate bowl and the breadcrumbs into another bowl. Brush the inside edges of the pocket of each breast with beaten egg and press together to seal. Turn each breast in the flour, brush off any excess, then dip into the beaten eggs and finally roll in the breadcrumbs to coat.

4 Heat the sunflower oil in a large frying pan over a medium heat, add the chicken and cook for 2 minutes on each side or until golden. Transfer to a large baking tray, place in an oven preheated to 180°C/Gas Mark 4 and bake for 20 minutes, until cooked through. Drizzle the pancetta with a little olive oil and add it to the baking tray after the chicken has been in the oven for about 10 minutes. Cook the pancetta until crisp.

5 For the salad, put the oil, vinegar, parsley and some salt and pepper into a large bowl and whisk together. Add the diced tomatoes, lettuce and herbs and toss gently with the dressing. Serve with the cooked chicken and pancetta.

CHICKEN THIGHS WITH HARISSA, TOMATO AND CHICKPEAS

Harissa is a North African spice paste. I like to make my own and add a generous amount to this recipe, but I've suggested using just half the quantity given below — it's incredibly hot!

Serves 4

1 tablespoon coriander seeds, crushed

2 teaspoons cumin seeds, crushed

seeds from 6 green cardamom pods

1 tablespoon groundnut oil

1 teaspoon coarse sea salt

3 tablespoons olive oil

8 chicken thighs or other joints, skin on

1 large Spanish onion, sliced

300ml chicken stock

1 tablespoon tomato purée

400g can of chickpeas, drained

4 tablespoons sultanas

4 tomatoes, skinned (see page 278, step 1), deseeded and cut into strips

a large handful of coriander, roughly chopped, plus extra to garnish

sea salt and black pepper

For the harissa:

100g red chillies, deseeded

3 garlic cloves, peeled

1 tablespoon coriander leaves

1½ tablespoons caster sugar

1½ tablespoons tomato purée

1 tablespoon olive oil

¼ teaspoon ground cumin

1 Make the harissa. Put all the ingredients into a food processor with some salt and process to make a chunky paste. Set aside.

2 Crush the coriander, cumin and cardamom seeds with a mortar and pestle. Mix the crushed spices with the groundnut oil and coarse sea salt. Rub into the chicken joints.

3 Heat the olive oil in a large frying pan, add the chicken and cook until browned on all sides. Remove from the pan and set aside. Add the onion and cook until softened. Return the chicken to the pan and add the stock, tomato purée and half the harissa (store the remainder in an airtight jar in the fridge for a few days). Stir in the chickpeas, sultanas and half the tomato strips. Bring to the boil, then cover the pan, reduce the heat and simmer for 25 minutes, turning the chicken over halfway through cooking.

4 Remove the chicken and transfer to a plate. Skim off the oil from the sauce and add the remaining tomato strips. Simmer until the sauce reduces and starts to thicken slightly. Return the chicken to the pan, taste for seasoning and stir in the coriander. Serve garnished with extra coriander and accompanied by rice.

GAME

Game is a seasonal food but very plentiful when
it's around. Game animals and birds eat a
natural diet and are so wonderfully lean and
healthy. However, because they contain very little
fat, they can end up tough and dry unless you
cook them correctly. The most important thing is
not to overcook them. When roasting or searing
white-meat game, such as partridge, pheasant and
rabbit, make sure they are pink but just cooked
through. Red-meat game, such as hare and
venison, are best served rare. Early in the season,
game is delicious roasted; later in the season, it is
usually best cooked slowly in a casserole.

There's only one way of dealing with a nice young partridge and that is to roast it. You prepare them by trussing, which is easy once you know how, and then searing prior to a quick roast at a high temperature. A portion is normally one bird per person.

~ ROAST PARTRIDGE ~

with cabbage, bacon and apple

To truss the partridge, follow steps 1 to 4

SERVES 4

4 oven-ready partridge

4 sprigs of thyme

2 tablespoons olive oil, plus a drizzle

4 rashers of streaky bacon

2 teaspoons unsalted butter

½ small onion, roughly chopped

1 small carrot, peeled and roughly chopped

1 celery stick, roughly chopped

25g caster sugar

200ml red wine

300ml chicken stock

2 teaspoons dried tarragon

zest of ½ orange, taken off in long strips with a peeler

1 tablespoon tomato purée

1 teaspoon coarse sea salt

2 tablespoons Grand Marnier

Beurre Manié (see page 70, tips), made with 15g soft unsalted butter and 15g plain flour) (optional)

sea salt and black pepper

FOR THE CABBAGE, BACON AND APPLE:

80g unsalted butter

2 Granny Smith apples, peeled, cored and diced

4 rashers of back bacon, chopped

1 Savoy cabbage

1 Run around the wishbone of each bird with the point of a small knife, then pull it out.

2 Cut a long length of butcher's string and use to tie the drumsticks together. Knot it and leave 2 long ends of string.

3 Take each of these around a thigh, pass them underneath the bird, cross the strings and then bring them up around the wishbone end.

4 Tie the ends together tightly to plump the bird up.

5 Season the inside and outside of each partridge with salt and pepper.

6 Put a sprig of thyme into the cavity of each bird, then cover and leave in the fridge until ready to cook.

7 To cook the partridge, heat the 2 tablespoons oil in a frying pan, add the partridge and brown on all sides over a high heat.

8 Cut each rasher of bacon in half, then lay 2 pieces over the breast of each bird.

9 Transfer the birds to a large roasting tin and place in an oven preheated to 200°C/Gas Mark 6. Roast for 12 minutes.

10 Remove from the oven and leave to rest for 5 minutes.

11 Cut off the breasts and legs, then put them back into the roasting tin ready to return to the oven to finish cooking.

12 To make the sauce, heat a drizzle of olive oil with 1 teaspoon of the butter in a frying pan.

13 Add the carcasses from the cooked partridge, 2 at a time, with the onion, carrot and celery and cook until browned on all sides.

14 Add the sugar and wine and simmer until reduced by half.

15 Then add the stock, tarragon, orange zest, tomato purée and salt and simmer until reduced by half again.

16 Pass through a fine sieve into a saucepan. Bring to a simmer and add the Grand Marnier.

17 Then whisk in the *beurre manié* a small piece at a time if the sauce needs thickening. Taste for seasoning. Keep warm.

18 For the cabbage, bacon and apple, melt 50g of the butter in a frying pan, add the apple and cook until browned. Remove from the pan.

19 Add the bacon and cook until browned. Return the apple to the pan and cook for a further 2 minutes. Set the pan aside off the heat.

20 Remove the stalk from the cabbage, then roll up the leaves and cut into 5mm-thick slices.

21 Cook in a large saucepan of boiling water for 1 minute, then drain well – it needs to be quite dry.

22 Add the cabbage to the bacon and apple, heat and toss with the remaining 30g butter. Season with salt and pepper.

23 When ready to serve, put the partridge breasts and legs back in the oven at 200°C/Gas Mark 6 for about 5 minutes, until heated through.

24 Whisk the remaining teaspoon of butter into the sauce. Serve 2 partridge breasts and 2 legs to each person with some sauce spooned around, together with the cabbage, bacon and apple.

roast partridge variations

Roast Partridge with Indian Spices – game works surprisingly well with Indian spices. Try rubbing ground spices on the birds before roasting – cumin, coriander, chilli etc. Omit the sauce and serve with yoghurt seasoned with plenty of chopped mint.

Roast Partridge with Star Anise – put a lightly crushed star anise pod and a few crushed peppercorns in the cavity of each bird to give a subtle flavour and aroma.

Roast Partridge with Beetroot – instead of the cabbage, serve with the Roast Beetroot on page 25.

Roast Grouse or Pheasant – grouse and pheasant can be cooked in the same way, though pheasants will need roasting for another 10 minutes.

TIPS AND IDEAS

■ All game birds, with the exeption of Snipe, can be prepared in the same way as the partridge.

■ Trussing the birds plumps up the breast when you put the string behind it. It also keeps them neat and tidy. They look like little soldiers all lined up in the dish.

■ The reason for taking the wishbone out is so you don't lose any meat later when you remove the breasts.

■ Make sure you brown the skin well in the frying pan; it gives a good texture and also tastes better.

■ The bacon helps keep the birds moist. I like to serve it with them as a garnish.

■ Ideally, while the birds are in the oven, you would cook them for 5 minutes on one side, then lay them on the other side and cook for another 5 minutes. Finally turn them right-side up and leave to finish. This helps keep them moist.

■ The birds can be roasted up to 3 hours in advance, as long as you are careful not to overcook them. This makes life so much easier for the cook.

■ Cooking the birds in advance also gives you time to make the sauce. Be sure to reduce it well to concentrate the flavours – by allowing yourself plenty of time to do it, you can get it how you want it.

■ Resting is as important as the cooking. It helps the meat to relax and become tender. So roasting the birds 3 hours in advance can be positively beneficial.

■ The cabbage can also be cooked well in advance. The trick is to slightly undercook everything if you are reheating it later.

■ *Beurre manié* is equal quantities of soft butter and plain flour beaten together. Shape the mixture into a log and keep it in the fridge, wrapped in cling film, for up to 3 weeks. You can slice off little pieces and whisk them into soups, sauces and stews to thicken them.

■ If you live in the country, you may find game gets very cheap in season. Buy some to store in your freezer, then you can enjoy it all year round, especially in terrines.

■ Partridge works well in most recipes that work with chicken.

■ Use leftover game carcasses to make wonderful stock.

PARTRIDGE WITH FRESH BLACKBERRIES

A wonderfully decorative dish, this makes the most of the fact that blackberries are around at the beginning of the game season.

Serves 4

4 oven-ready partridge

8 rashers of streaky bacon

2 tablespoons olive oil

1 small leek, finely diced

1 carrot, peeled and finely diced

1 onion, finely diced

2 garlic cloves, diced

3 sprigs of thyme

1 tablespoon plain flour

325ml red wine

1 litre chicken stock or game stock

4 bay leaves

200ml double cream

3 tablespoons blackcurrant cordial

250g blackberries

sea salt and black pepper

1 Run the point of a small knife around the wishbone of each bird, then pull it out (see page 67). Remove the backbone from each partridge by cutting along both sides of the backbone with a sharp boning knife and removing it. Now cut each partridge into 4 parts: 2 breasts with wings and 2 legs.

2 Place the bacon between 2 sheets of greaseproof paper and run a rolling pin over them so that the rashers become nice and thin. Cut them in half lengthways. Wrap a piece of bacon around each partridge joint and secure with a cocktail stick.

3 Heat a little olive oil in a large frying pan over a medium heat, add the partridge pieces and brown all over. Transfer them to a casserole.

4 Put a little more oil in the pan, add the leek, carrot, onion, garlic and thyme and cook until lightly browned. Sprinkle over the flour and stir well. Transfer to the casserole with the partridge.

5 Pour the wine into the frying pan and stir to dissolve any sediment in the bottom of the pan. Simmer to reduce by half, then add the liquid to the casserole. Pour in the stock so that it almost covers the partridge pieces, leaving a bit of the meat exposed. Stir carefully, so as not to dislodge the bacon, then add the bay leaves. Place the casserole in an oven preheated to 180°C/Gas Mark 4 and cook for 45 minutes.

6 Check to see if the partridge pieces are tender enough after 40 minutes by inserting a sharp knife, which should come out easily. If ready, transfer the pieces to a warmed serving dish. Strain the vegetables through a sieve, reserving the liquid, and pour the liquid back into the casserole. Discard the vegetables or use them to make a soup. Place the casserole over a medium heat, bring to a simmer and reduce the liquid by two-thirds. This will take about 15–20 minutes.

7 Add the cream and blackcurrant cordial to the sauce and simmer for another 5 minutes, stirring. Season well with salt and pepper. Return the partridge pieces to the casserole with the sauce. Scatter with the fresh blackberries and serve.

SPATCHCOCKED PARTRIDGE WITH LEMON AND GARLIC AND THIN CHIPS

Spatchcocking a bird means removing the wishbone and backbone, then pressing down to flatten it. To keep it flat, you have to skewer it through from the shoulder to the leg. It's normally done with chicken but I thought partridge would be wonderful — and it was!

Serves 4

4 oven-ready partridge

juice and grated zest of 2 lemons

2 garlic cloves, crushed

5 tablespoons olive oil

1 tablespoon coarse sea salt

1 teaspoon coarsely ground black pepper

lemon wedges, to serve

For the thin chips:

1kg all-purpose potatoes, such as Maris Piper

sunflower oil for deep-frying

sea salt and white pepper

1 First remove the wishbones: run around the wishbone of each partridge with the point of a small knife, then pull it out. Remove the backbones by cutting down and along both sides and pressing through the ribs. Spatchcock the partridges by pressing them down with your hands, skin-side up, to spread them out. I like to push 2 long skewers diagonally through each partridge to secure them, which makes them easier to handle.

2 Sprinkle the lemon juice and zest, garlic and 4 tablespoons of the olive oil over the partridge. Season with the salt and pepper and rub in well all over. Cover and leave to marinate in the fridge for at least 1 hour, longer if possible.

3 To make the chips, peel the potatoes, cut them into slices 5mm thick and then into 5mm-thick lengths. Rinse under cold running water, then dry them well on kitchen paper.

4 Heat some sunflower oil in a deep-fat fryer or a deep saucepan to 150°C, carefully add the potatoes and fry in small batches for 5–6 minutes, until pale golden brown. Remove and drain well on kitchen paper (this part can be done in advance). Increase the oil temperature to 180°C, then return the chips to the oil in batches and cook very briefly until deep golden brown. Drain on kitchen paper and season with salt and white pepper.

5 Meanwhile, cook the partridges. Heat the remaining olive oil in a large frying pan and fry each partridge, skin-side down, until pale golden brown, then transfer them to 2 roasting trays. Place in an oven preheated to 180°C/Gas Mark 4 and roast for 18–20 minutes, until golden brown all over and just pink inside. Remove from the oven and leave to rest for 3 minutes.

6 Serve with the chips and lemon wedges.

A crown is the bird with the legs and backbone removed, so you roast the breasts on the remaining carcass. This recipe uses pheasant, but you can prepare any bird in the same way. I love the combination of earthy pheasants, lentils and chestnuts here. A proper winter dish.

ROAST CROWN OF PHEASANT

on lentils and chestnuts

To prepare the crowns, follow steps 1 to 8

SERVES 4

2 oven-ready pheasants

4 tablespoons olive oil, plus a drizzle

1 garlic clove, crushed

a knob of unsalted butter

sea salt and black pepper

chopped parsley, to garnish

FOR THE LENTILS:

2 tablespoons olive oil

2 rashers of streaky bacon, finely chopped

1 small onion, finely chopped

2 garlic cloves, finely chopped

750ml chicken or pheasant stock

150g Puy lentils

200g peeled and cooked chestnuts, roughly chopped

2 tablespoons finely chopped curly parsley

1 tablespoon green peppercorns

50ml double cream

1 First prepare the pheasant crowns. Run around the wishbone of each bird with the point of a small knife, then pull it out.

2 Cut off the wing joints and discard.

3 To remove the leg, cut through the skin between the leg and the carcass.

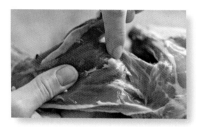

4 Then with your hand, twist the thigh back to click it out of its socket.

5 Cut around the socket and remove, taking the oyster (the round piece of meat at the end of the thigh bone where it joins the body) with the leg.

6 Place each leg skin-side down and feel with your thumb for the joint dividing the thigh and drumstick. Cut through the joint.

7 With the cavity towards you, cut down the length of each bird with poultry sheers. Remove the backbone from the carcass.

8 What you have now is the crown – the 2 breasts. Keep the carcass to use for stock.

9 Mix the 4 tablespoons oil, garlic and 1 teaspoon salt together.

10 Rub into the crowns, then place on a tray, cover and leave in the fridge until ready to cook.

11 For the lentils, heat the oil in a saucepan, add the bacon and onion and cook over a medium heat for a couple of minutes.

12 Add the garlic, stock and lentils, bring to the boil and simmer for about 20 minutes, until all the liquid has been absorbed.

roast crown of pheasant variations

Roast Crown of Pheasant with Pearl Barley – melt 20g unsalted butter in a pan, add 2 finely chopped shallots, 1 finely chopped leek and 2 finely chopped celery sticks and cook gently until softened. Stir in 200g pearl barley, then pour in 500ml chicken stock and bring to the boil. Cover and simmer for about 1 hour, until the barley is tender and the stock has been absorbed, adding more stock if necessary. Stir in 150ml double cream and 2 tablespoons chopped tarragon and cook for another 5 minutes, then season well. Serve with the pheasant (see pages 74–76) instead of the lentils.

Roast Crown of Pheasant with Red Wine Risotto – serve the pheasant (see pages 74–76) with a red wine risotto made following the instructions on page 88 and using 30g unsalted butter, 1 finely chopped onion instead of the leeks, 250g Arborio rice, 2 raw beetroot, finely diced and added with the rice, 300ml red wine boiled to reduce by a third and then added after the rice and beetroot, and 800ml chicken stock. Finish by mixing in 40g unsalted butter, 50g freshly grated Parmesan cheese and a handful of chopped flat-leaf parsley.

PHEASANT CASSEROLE

Serves 4

2 hen pheasants

plain flour for dusting

50g unsalted butter

2 tablespoons olive oil

4 rashers of streaky bacon, cut into 2cm pieces

250g onions, sliced

2 celery sticks, chopped

2 garlic cloves, finely chopped

100g raisins

300ml red wine (optional)

700ml chicken stock or game stock

sea salt and black pepper

1 Joint the pheasants into 8 pieces (see page 55). Set the drumsticks aside (you could use them to make stock). Dust the thigh and breast pieces lightly with flour, shaking off any excess.

2 Heat half the butter and oil in a large frying pan over a medium heat, add the pheasant pieces in batches and cook until browned all over. Once browned, transfer to a large casserole.

3 Add the bacon to the frying pan, cook until browned and transfer to the casserole. Heat the rest of the butter and oil in the frying pan, add the sliced onions and cook until golden. Transfer to the casserole.

4 Add the celery, garlic and raisins and cook for 1 minute, then add the red wine, if using, and boil until reduced by a third. Stir well and transfer to the casserole. Add the stock, bring to a simmer and stir.

5 Cover with a lid and place the casserole in an oven preheated to 180°C/Gas Mark 4. Cook for 20 minutes, then reduce the temperature to 150°C/Gas Mark 2 and cook for a further 50 minutes, until the birds are tender. Remove the pheasant from the casserole and set aside to rest, keeping it warm. Bring the liquid in the casserole to a simmer and cook until it starts to thicken slightly. Season well with salt and pepper. Return the pheasant to the casserole and serve with Creamed Potatoes (see page 86).

PHEASANT PANCAKES WITH CHEESE SAUCE

A friend of mine, Diana, devised this dish to use up leftover pheasant. It was absolutely wonderful and I'm so pleased to include it here. It's a good way to get children to eat pheasant if they're not generally keen on game.

Serves 4

40g unsalted butter, plus extra for greasing

150g onions, finely chopped

250g button mushrooms, chopped

the meat of 1 cooked pheasant (or however much leftover pheasant you have), minced or finely chopped

1 quantity of White Sauce (see page 252)

250g Gruyère or Cheddar cheese, grated

1 quantity of Pancakes (see pages 168–170)

sea salt and black pepper

1 Melt the butter in a large frying pan, add the onions, and cook, stirring occasionally, until softened, then add the mushrooms and cook for a few more minutes. Add the onion and mushrooms to the chopped pheasant in a bowl and mix together well. Season with salt and pepper.

2 Gently reheat the white sauce, if necessary. Add the cheese, reserving a little for sprinkling later, and stir until melted.

3 Add 2 tablespoons of the sauce to the pheasant mixture.

4 Grease an ovenproof gratin dish with butter. Spoon some of the pheasant mixture on to the centre of each pancake and roll it up. Place the pancakes in the gratin dish. Pour the rest of the cheese sauce over the top and sprinkle over the remaining cheese. Place in an oven preheated to 180°C/Gas Mark 4 and bake for 20–25 minutes, until golden brown. Serve immediately.

SEARED PHEASANT BREASTS WITH WILD MUSHROOMS AND CRÈME FRAÎCHE

Serves 4

4 pheasant breasts, preferably from hen pheasants

olive oil

400g wild mushrooms, such as girolles, chanterelles, ceps, black trumpet or oyster mushrooms

60g unsalted butter

4 sprigs of thyme

200ml chicken stock or game stock

200ml crème fraîche

2 teaspoons sugar

2 rounded tablespoons finely chopped curly parsley

sea salt and black pepper

1 Remove any sinew from the breasts with a sharp knife and season with salt and pepper on both sides. Heat a little oil in a large frying pan over a high heat and brown the pheasant breasts, skin-side down, for 1 minute. Turn them over and brown the other side, then remove and set aside.

2 To prepare the wild mushrooms, trim off any hard stalks and wipe the mushrooms clean with damp kitchen paper. Cut them in half or quarters lengthways.

3 Melt the butter in the frying pan, add the mushrooms and thyme and cook gently for 5 minutes. Add the stock, continue cooking for 2 minutes, then stir in the crème fraîche and sugar. Continue cooking for 5 minutes over a low heat, then stir in the parsley and season with salt and pepper. Set aside and keep warm.

4 Place the pheasant breasts on a roasting tray and cook in an oven preheated to 190°C/Gas Mark 5 for about 5 minutes. They should be just pink inside, not rare. Allow to rest for 5 minutes, adding any juices released from the pheasant to the mushrooms. Serve the pheasant breasts on the mushrooms.

VENISON CARPACCIO WITH CELERIAC SPAGHETTI, PARMESAN AND BALSAMIC VINEGAR

This is one of my favourite recipes ever. Carpaccio is traditionally made with beef but venison is a wonderful substitute. For me, the only way to eat red game is extremely rare, so carpaccio simply takes it one step further.

Serves 4

500g venison loin

250g celeriac, peeled and cut into thin strips

juice of ½ lemon

2 teaspoons mayonnaise

1 teaspoon wholegrain mustard

80g Parmesan cheese, in one piece

6 tablespoons extra virgin olive oil

2 tablespoons balsamic vinegar

sea salt and black pepper

micro herbs or small salad leaves, to garnish

1 Slice the loin of venison as thinly as possible. Put 2 slices on a large piece of cling film and place another piece of cling film on top. Roll out the venison with a rolling pin as gently as you can, until it becomes as thin as Parma ham. Set aside, still wrapped in the cling film, and repeat the process with the remaining venison.

2 Place the celeriac in a bowl with the lemon juice, mayonnaise and mustard, season to taste and mix well. Set aside.

3 Use a potato peeler to peel the Parmesan into thin shavings.

4 Put the olive oil and balsamic vinegar into a bowl, whisk well and season with salt and pepper.

5 Two hours before serving, carefully lift the venison off the cling film and put it on individual serving plates, spreading it out to cover the whole plate. Brush the oil and vinegar mixture over the venison and season with salt. Place a large metal ring or pastry cutter in the centre of the each plate, fill it with celeriac and remove the ring to create a small pile. Keep cool until required.

6 Just before serving, scatter the Parmesan strips and micro herbs or small salad leaves over the venison.

Carpaccio variations

Beef carpaccio – Place 400g beef fillet in the freezer for 2 hours, then remove it and slice it finely. Arrange on serving plates, season with sea salt and coarsely ground black pepper and drizzle with extra virgin olive oil. Scatter with 50g Parmesan cheese shavings and serve.

Wild duck carpaccio with basil pesto – Remove all the skin and sinew from 4 wild duck breasts. Slice thinly, place each slice between cling film, roll out and place on serving plates as for the venison. Drizzle with 4 tablespoons Pesto (see page 174) and 2 tablespoons extra virgin olive oil. Sprinkle with sea salt, black pepper and basil leaves.

WILD DUCK WITH RED CABBAGE AND PORT AND ROWAN SAUCE

Serves 4

2 wild ducks

3 tablespoons olive oil

300g fresh spinach

a pinch of freshly grated nutmeg

30g unsalted butter

sea salt and black pepper

For the red cabbage:

90g unsalted butter

180g onions, finely chopped

2 rashers of smoked streaky bacon, diced

½ red cabbage, very finely shredded

400g raw beetroot, finely diced

2 apples, peeled, cored and diced

2 tablespoons honey

50ml red wine vinegar

100ml red wine

300ml chicken stock

For the port and rowan sauce:

olive oil

15g unsalted butter

1 rasher of smoked streaky bacon, finely chopped

50g leek, finely chopped

300ml red wine

1 rounded tablespoon rowan jelly

300ml game stock or chicken stock

120ml port

1 Joint the ducks as instructed on page 55, steps 1–7.

2 Start with the red cabbage. Melt the butter in a saucepan over a low heat, add the onion and cook gently until softened. Add the bacon, cook for 1 minute, then add the red cabbage, beetroot, apples, honey, vinegar, red wine and stock. Cover and cook over a very low heat for 1½ hours, stirring occasionally. Season with salt and plenty of pepper, then cook for a further 30 minutes. This can be prepared up to 2 days in advance.

3 For the sauce, heat a little oil in a large pan and fry the duck legs, wings and bones over a high heat until well browned. Melt the butter in the pan, add the bacon and leek and cook over a fairly high heat for 15 minutes, stirring regularly. Add the red wine and rowan jelly and boil until the liquid is reduced to 2 tablespoons. Add the stock and boil until reduced to a third, then remove the duck with tongs and discard. Strain the liquid through a sieve into a clean pan, season with salt and pepper, add the port and bring back to the boil briefly. This can be done well in advance.

4 Heat 1 tablespoon of the olive oil in a large pan and add the spinach. Cook until wilted, drain well and season with grated nutmeg, salt and pepper. Set aside and keep warm.

5 Remove the skin from the duck breasts. Heat the remaining oil in an ovenproof frying pan and brown the breasts on both sides over a high heat for 1 minute. Add the butter and place in an oven preheated to 200°C/Gas Mark 6 for 3 minutes, until cooked very rare. Remove and allow it to rest in a warm place for 10 minutes.

6 Slice each duck breast into 3 lengthways, then serve with the spinach and red cabbage, pouring the sauce around.

MEAT

Meat doesn't have to be expensive but it must
be good quality, so always choose the best meat
you can afford. When buying meat, look for nice
creamy fat rather than bright-white fat, which
is a sign of intensive farming. Creamy fat is an
indication that an animal has had a good life —
and that it will taste better. Cheaper cuts of meat
invariably need to be cooked for longer than the
prime cuts and, although you can't beat a rib of
beef or rack of pork, it has to be said that in some
instances cheaper cuts have the best flavour.

Meat cooked on the bone is always so much more flavoursome than boned pieces. Cleaning the bones of the rack might seem unnecessary but it looks so much prettier and your guests will be very impressed.

ROAST RACK OF PORK

with apple sauce

To prepare the rack of pork, follow steps 1 to 5

SERVES 6

a 6- or 7-chop rack of pork, weighing about 1.4kg (at room temperature)

2 teaspoons coarse sea salt

a drizzle of olive oil

2 Spanish onions, sliced

8 sprigs of thyme or 1 tablespoon dried thyme

200ml Madeira

150ml pork or chicken stock

sea salt and coarsely ground black pepper

FOR THE APPLE SAUCE:

5 large Cox's apples, peeled, cored and sliced (about 600g prepared weight)

100ml white wine vinegar

120g granulated sugar

2 cloves

30g unsalted butter

1 Using a large, sharp knife, cut the skin off the rack of pork, leaving the fat on the meat. Reserve the skin.

2 Using a small, sharp knife, cut off the flesh between the bones.

3 Clean the bones well by scraping hard against the bone with your knife.

4 Rub the bones with a cloth to ensure they are completely clean.

5 Score the fat into diamond shapes by cutting lines diagonally one way and then the other way, being careful not to cut the meat.

6 Rub the pork all over with the coarse sea salt and some coarsely ground black pepper.

7 Heat the oil in a large frying pan, add the pork and cook over a medium heat until nicely caramelised all over.

8 Put the onions and thyme in a roasting tin and lay the pork on top. Put into an oven preheated to 200°C/Gas Mark 6 and roast for 30 minutes.

9 Turn the oven down to 150°C/Gas Mark 2. Lay the pork skin on a rack over a roasting tin. Add to the oven. Roast for a further 1 hour 10 minutes.

10 Meanwhile, make the apple sauce (or make this the day before). Put the apples into a saucepan with the vinegar, sugar and cloves.

11 Cook over a low heat, uncovered, for about 20 minutes until the apples are soft. If the mixture becomes dry, just add a little water.

12 Beat in the butter and season the apple sauce with salt.

13 Check that the pork is done by inserting a fine knife in the centre; the juices should run clear. Remove from the oven and transfer to a board.

14 Leave the pork to rest for at least 15 minutes While it is resting, allow the skin to crisp in the oven, turning the temperature up to 190°C/Gas Mark 5. This will take about 15–20 minutes.

15 Strain the onions and pan juices through a sieve into a bowl, removing any burnt bits.

16 Skim off any fat and reserve the dark juices for adding to the gravy.

17 Remove the thyme, then purée the onions in a food processor or with a hand blender and also reserve for the gravy.

18 Combine any juices that run from the pork with the other reserved meat juices and add to the puréed onions.

19 To make the gravy, add the Madeira to the roasting tin.

20 Bring to a simmer, stirring and scraping the base of the tin to deglaze it.

21 Gradually stir in the onion purée.

22 Add the stock and cook for 5 minutes, until reduced to a well-flavoured gravy.

23 Strain through a fine sieve into a small saucepan. Adjust the seasoning and reheat gently.

24 Break the crackling into strips. Cut the rack into separate chops and serve one per person, accompanied by the gravy, crackling and apple sauce.

roast rack of pork variations

Marinated Roast Rack of Pork – mix together 100ml olive oil, 2 teaspoons sea salt, 1 crushed garlic clove, the needles from 3 sprigs of rosemary and the juice and grated zest of 1 lemon. Rub this mixture into the pork after scoring the fat and leave to marinate overnight. Roast the pork following the recipe on pages 96–98.

Roast Rack of Pork with Pancetta – follow the recipe on pages 96–98, wrapping 12 slices of pancetta over the rack before roasting.

Roast Rack of Pork with Seared Apples – fry some sliced apples in unsalted butter until tender and lightly coloured, then remove from the heat and stir in 2 tablespoons redcurrant jelly. Transfer to a bowl and serve with the roast rack of pork (see pages 96–98) instead of the apple sauce.

TIPS AND IDEAS

■ Remember to weigh the pork before cooking. Pigs come in all sizes and therefore so do pork racks. A good rule is to cook for 25–30 minutes per 450g.

■ If you have a meat thermometer, cook the pork till it registers 65°C in the centre. Otherwise, insert a fine knife into the centre and check that the juices run clear. Although some restaurants now serve pork pink, I feel that, like undercooked chicken, it's just plain wrong.

■ I take the skin off the pork to make crackling. It often curls in the oven, so a good tip is to weave a skewer in and out of it before you cook it, so it stays flat.

■ Adding vinegar to the apple sauce gives a lovely sweet and sour effect, which works well with the sweetness of the apples. You could omit it if you prefer.

■ It is absolutely essential to rest the meat for at least 15 minutes after roasting – this completes the cooking and ensures it is tender and succulent.

■ Making the gravy in the pan in which the pork was cooked means you can include all the lovely, caramelised juices from the meat. If there are any burnt bits, just scrape them out and discard them.

■ If you don't have any Madeira wine, you can substitute sweet sherry or Marsala.

Guidelines for roasting joints of meat

	Cooking time per 450g	Internal temperature	Resting time
Beef or lamb, rare	10–12 minutes	50°C (60°C in the thickest part)	30–40 minutes
Beef or lamb, medium	15–18 minutes	60°C	30–40 minutes
Beef or lamb, well done	20–25 minutes	75°C	30–40 minutes
Pork, medium rare	20 minutes	60°C	25 minutes
Pork, medium	25 minutes	65°C	25 minutes
Pork, well done	25–30 minutes	70°C	25 minutes
Veal	15–18 minutes	65°C	30 minutes

TENDERLOIN OF PORK WRAPPED IN HERBS

This is a really quick and easy dish, but it does help if you can chill the meat for 4 hours in the fridge first to get a good round shape. If you're in a rush, this isn't absolutely necessary. I love this served with cauliflower cheese.

Serves 4

3 tablespoons finely chopped tarragon

2 tablespoons finely chopped thyme

2 tablespoons finely chopped curly parsley

1 large pork tenderloin, sinews removed

2 tablespoons olive oil

sea salt and black pepper

1 In a shallow dish, mix the tarragon, thyme and parsley and season with salt and pepper. Cut the pork tenderloin into 2 neat pieces, season with salt and pepper and roll both pieces in the herbs. Wrap each piece tightly in cling film and chill in the fridge for at least 4 hours.

2 Heat the oil in an ovenproof frying pan over a medium heat. Remove the cling film from the pork, add the pork pieces to the pan and lightly brown on all sides. Place in an oven preheated to 200°C/Gas Mark 6 and cook for approximately 10 minutes; when the pork is done, it should feel quite firm to the touch. Remove, allow to rest for at least 10 minutes and then slice to serve.

SLOW-COOKED KNUCKLE OF GAMMON WITH STAR ANISE, GINGER AND SOY

Knuckle of gammon is such good value and full of flavour. In this recipe, you end up with a rich, sticky, aromatic coating and deliciously tender meat.

Serves 4

2kg gammon knuckle

1 tablespoon olive oil

1 litre chicken stock

1 large onion, thinly sliced

2cm piece of fresh ginger, thinly sliced

6 star anise pods

2 tablespoons caster sugar

6 tablespoons soy sauce

1 teaspoon coarse sea salt

1 Place the gammon knuckle in a large pan, cover with cold water and bring to the boil. Simmer for 30 minutes, then drain.

2 Heat the oil in a large flameproof casserole, add the gammon and brown it on all sides. Add the chicken stock, onion, ginger, star anise, sugar, soy sauce and salt and bring to a simmer. Cover the casserole and place in an oven preheated to 200°C/Gas Mark 6 and cook for 30 minutes, then turn the oven down to 140°C/Gas Mark 1 and cook for a further 2½ hours, turning the gammon every 30 minutes.

3 Remove the gammon from the casserole and allow to rest for 20 minutes. Put the casserole on the hob and boil the liquid until reduced to a third of its original volume; it should have a slightly sticky, sauce-like consistency. Carve the gammon and pour the sauce around. Serve with buttered purple sprouting broccoli.

There is nothing nicer than a sizzling sausage and they are great fun to make. You should be able to order the skins from a good butcher, but even if you don't have any you can just shape the mixture into sausages and fry it.

PORK SAUSAGES

with caramelised onion

To make the sausages, follow steps 1 to 12

SERVES 4

1kg belly pork, finely minced

50g fresh white breadcrumbs

3 tablespoons finely chopped parsley (optional)

2 teaspoons thyme leaves

2 teaspoons fine sea salt, or to taste

2 teaspoons black pepper

½ teaspoon cayenne pepper

2 tablespoons milk

a drizzle of olive oil

natural sausage casings, preferably hog (if they are salted, soak in cold water for 2 hours, then rinse)

15g lard or 1 tablespoon olive oil

FOR THE CARAMELISED ONION:

50g unsalted butter

2 tablespoons olive oil

5 red onions, thinly sliced

40g caster sugar

sea salt and black pepper

1 First make the sausage filling. Put the pork, breadcrumbs, herbs, salt, pepper, cayenne and milk into a bowl and mix well.

2 To check the seasoning, form a little of the mixture into a small patty. Heat the drizzle of olive oil in a small frying pan.

3 Add the patty and fry until cooked through. Taste and add more seasoning to the remaining mixture if needed.

4 To put the sausage meat into the casings, roll a length of sausage casing over the nozzle of the sausage maker.

5 Leave the end few centimetres free and tie in a knot.

6 Load your sausage maker with the filling.

7 With one hand half on the nozzle and half on the casing, slowly feed the sausage meat into the casing.

8 Continue to feed the sausage meat into the casing, controlling the flow by varying the pressure on the nozzle so that you fill the casing evenly.

9 You will now have one long sausage. Tie a knot in the free end.

10 Lay the sausage out on the work surface. Using your thumb and forefinger, pinch the mixture at evenly spaced points to divide the sausage into 12 sections.

11 Twist one sausage up, the next down and the final one up again, to divide into 3 links.

12 Keep going until you have 12 sausages. Place the sausages in the fridge and leave them to rest for at least 1 hour before you fry them.

13 For the caramelised onion, melt the butter with the oil in a large frying pan.

14 Add the onions and cook over a low heat for 30 minutes, stirring occasionally, until completely soft. Turn the heat up a little and add the sugar.

15 Cook for a further 5–10 minutes, until very lightly caramelised. Season well and leave to cool. Cover and refrigerate until required.

16 When ready to cook the sausages, put the caramelised onion into a small saucepan and heat gently.

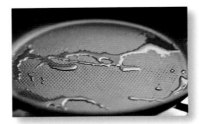

17 Heat the lard or olive oil in a large frying pan.

18 Add the sausages and cook in batches over a medium heat for about 15 minutes, until browned all over and cooked through. Serve with the caramelised onion.

TIPS AND IDEAS

■ I always use natural rather than synthetic skins but they can break, so you need to handle them gently.

■ If possible, rest the sausages for a day after making them – this gives them a chance to firm up.

■ When you tie sausages, try to tie in threes, like a butcher does. It's complicated but worth trying to get the knack.

■ If you don't want to make individual sausages, just do one long coil to make a Cumberland sausage – this is great on a barbecue.

■ If you're planning to make them regularly, it's worth getting a sausage-making kit.

■ Sausages will keep for a good 3 days in the fridge, and they freeze very well too. It's a good idea to make a big batch and freeze them.

■ Sausages are infinitely nicer fried than grilled or roasted – they are simply more succulent.

■ It's best not to prick sausages when cooking them or you will lose some of the lovely, flavoursome juices.

■ A little tip for cooking sausages is to wrap them in cling film, half cook them in a steamer, then finish them off in a frying pan. This stops the skins bursting and it also means you can part cook them well in advance.

pork sausage variations

Pork and Leek Sausages – finely chop the white part of 1 large leek and cook in a little butter until soft, then leave to cool. Follow the recipe on pages 104–105, adding the leek to the sausage mixture and omitting the milk.

Venison and Juniper Berry Sausages – mix together 500g finely minced venison shoulder, 450g minced pork shoulder, 3 teaspoons fine sea salt, 1 tablespoon juniper berries, finely crushed, 2 teaspoons freshly ground black peppercorns, 100g fresh white breadcrumbs and enough red wine to moisten. Use to make sausages, following the recipe on pages 104–105.

Beef Sausages – heat 2 tablespoons olive oil in a frying pan, add 150g very finely chopped onions and cook until soft. Leave to cool. Mix with 600g finely minced beef, 200g finely minced pork shoulder or belly pork, 2 finely chopped garlic cloves and 2 teaspoons each dried thyme, fine sea salt and black pepper. Use to make sausages, following the recipe on pages 104–105.

Lamb Sausages – heat 2 tablespoons olive oil in a frying pan, add 100g very finely chopped onions and cook until soft. Leave to cool. Mix with 700g finely minced lamb shoulder, 100g finely minced belly pork, 50g fresh white breadcrumbs, 2 tablespoons finely chopped thyme, 1 tablespoon each finely chopped mint and rosemary, 1 rounded tablespoon redcurrant jelly, 3 teaspoons fine sea salt and 1 teaspoon black pepper. Use to make sausages, following the recipe on pages 104–105.

PORK SAUSAGES IN WHITE WINE

This is a lovely, warming family dish and you can use whatever sausages you like. Serve with French bread and mustard.

Serves 4

1 tablespoon olive oil

8 plump pork sausages

1 onion, sliced

2 garlic cloves, finely chopped

750ml chicken stock

1 tablespoon tomato purée

500g waxy potatoes, peeled and halved

2 tablespoons chopped mixed herbs, such as marjoram, thyme and rosemary

1 tablespoon finely chopped flat-leaf parsley

sea salt and black pepper

1 Heat the oil in a frying pan, add the sausages and brown them all over. Remove from the pan and leave to cool slightly. Add the onion and garlic to the pan and cook until softened (this way you retain the flavour of the sausages from the pan).

2 Put the sausages and onion in a flameproof casserole along with all the rest of the ingredients except the parsley. Bring to a simmer, then cover and place in an oven preheated to 180°C/Gas Mark 4 and cook for 40 minutes. Remove from the oven, take out the sausages and potatoes and keep warm. Put the casserole on the hob, bring the liquid to the boil and simmer until reduced by half. Season with salt and pepper. Return the sausages and potatoes to the casserole and sprinkle with the chopped parsley.

PORK SAUSAGES WITH MUSHY BAKED BUTTER BEANS

This is what I call real comfort food. Children invariably adore it.

Serves 4

250g dried butter beans, soaked in cold water overnight

1 carrot, peeled and cut into chunks

1 onion, cut into quarters

1 celery stick, cut into chunks

1 bay leaf

2 sprigs of parsley

8 plump pork sausages

sea salt

For the sauce:

1 tablespoon olive oil

300g onions, finely chopped

4 garlic cloves, finely chopped

4 tablespoons tomato ketchup

2 tablespoons tomato purée

250g can of chopped tomatoes

2 tablespoons sugar

4 drops of Tabasco sauce

1 tablespoon Henderson's Relish or Worcestershire sauce

1 Drain the beans, put them in a large pan and cover with fresh water. Bring to the boil and cook for a couple of minutes before draining them again. Return them to the pan, cover with cold water and add the carrot, onion, celery, bay leaf and parsley. Stir, bring to the boil, then simmer for about 1½ hours or until just tender. Add a little more water if it is reducing too much. Once cooked, drain the beans and reserve 500ml of the cooking liquid.

2 Meanwhile, make the sauce. Heat the oil in a frying pan over a low heat. Add the onions and garlic and cook for 2 minutes, until softened. Add the remaining ingredients and the reserved bean water to the pan and cook gently for a further 10 minutes. Transfer to a blender and blitz until smooth.

3 Put the cooked beans in a large ovenproof dish along with the sauce and a pinch of salt. Cover, place in an oven preheated to 180°C/Gas Mark 4 and cook for 1 hour, reducing the temperature to 150°C/Gas Mark 2 after 30 minutes. Set aside until cool, then refrigerate until required.

4 Put the sausages on a baking tray and place in an oven preheated to 190°C/Gas Mark 5. Cook for 45 minutes, until nicely browned. Reheat the beans in an ovenproof dish at the same time as the sausages.

MEAT

THE BEST HAMBURGERS WITH PICKLED CUCUMBER AND BEETROOT SALAD

What I love about hamburgers is that you can use any meat at all to make them — pork, beef, lamb, chicken, whatever you like. The seasonings in this recipe give the burgers a deliciously piquant flavour.

Makes 4 large burgers

For the pickled cucumber:

1 large cucumber

2 teaspoons salt

2 tablespoons white wine vinegar

2 tablespoons caster sugar

For the beetroot salad:

4 beetroot, cooked and peeled

2½ tablespoons extra virgin olive oil

2 teaspoons balsamic vinegar

2 rounded tablespoons finely chopped curly parsley

sea salt and black pepper

For the burgers:

1 tablespoon olive oil, plus a drizzle

30g unsalted butter

150g onions, finely chopped

400g best-quality finely minced beef

4 small gherkins, finely chopped

2 tablespoons finely chopped curly parsley

1 garlic clove, finely chopped

1 teaspoon Worcestershire sauce

1 tablespoon tomato ketchup

a pinch of chilli powder

½ teaspoon black pepper

1 teaspoon fine sea salt

To serve:

4 rolls or baps, split in half

mayonnaise

1 Little Gem lettuce, shredded

4 vine-ripened tomatoes, sliced

1 Peel the cucumber and slice it, preferably on a mandoline. It should be very, very thin. Put it into a colander, sprinkle over the salt and allow it to sit for 30 minutes, then drain well. Put the cucumber into a bowl, add the vinegar and sugar and leave for 30 minutes.

2 Cut the cooked beetroot into 1cm dice. Put into a bowl and stir in the olive oil, balsamic vinegar and parsley. Season with salt and pepper.

3 For the burgers, heat the 1 tablespoon oil and butter in a non-stick frying pan, add the onions and cook gently until softened, without browning. Let Allow to cool. Put the beef, gherkins, parsley, garlic, Worcestershire sauce, ketchup, chilli powder, pepper and salt into a large bowl, add the cooked onion and mix well. To check the seasoning, make a tiny patty with a little of the mixture and fry it on both sides, then taste. Season the remaining mixture with more salt and pepper if necessary.

4 Shape the beef mixture into 4 hamburgers. A good way to do this is to put it into a deep metal ring, then remove the ring and press down a little with the palm of your hand. This gives a good round shape.

5 Wipe out the frying pan, add a drizzle of oil and place over a medium-high heat. When it is hot, add the hamburgers. Reduce the heat a little and cook for 4 minutes or until well browned underneath. Turn them over and cook for a further 4 minutes; they should still be pink inside. Transfer to a warm plate and leave to rest.

6 To serve the burgers, I like to fry the cut side of the rolls in the frying pan. Remove and spread with mayonnaise, top with the lettuce and tomatoes, then the hamburgers, add some more lettuce and tomato and finish with the tops of the rolls. Serve with the pickled cucumber and beetroot salad on the side.

OSSO BUCO WITH RISOTTO MILANESE

Osso buco is one of my favourite Italian dishes. The marrow contained in the shin bone is what makes it so spectacular. I like to take the meat off the bone to serve, but traditionally it is left on the bone — you can do this if you prefer.

Serves 4

4 thick slices of veal shin (make sure the bones still contain the marrow)

2 tablespoons plain flour, seasoned with salt

50g unsalted butter

3 tablespoons olive oil

1 onion, finely chopped

1 carrot, finely chopped

1 celery stick, finely chopped

4 tomatoes, chopped

a sprig of thyme

100ml white wine

about 800ml chicken stock

Beurre Manié (see page 70, tips), made with 15g soft unsalted butter and 15g plain flour (optional)

1 tablespoon caster sugar

sea salt and black pepper

For the gremolata:

grated zest of 2 lemons

4 tablespoons finely chopped flat-leaf parsley

1 garlic clove, finely chopped

For the risotto:

1 litre chicken stock

a large pinch of saffron strands

60g unsalted butter

1 small onion, finely chopped

250g Arborio rice

50g Parmesan cheese, freshly grated

1 Tie up each piece of veal shin with butcher's string like a parcel (this prevents the meat falling off the bone during cooking), then dust with the seasoned flour. Heat the butter and oil in a frying pan, add the veal and brown on both sides, then transfer to a large flameproof casserole.

2 Add the remaining 1 tablespoon oil to the pan, followed by the onion and cook until the onion is soft. Add the carrot, celery, tomatoes and thyme and cook for 3 minutes. Transfer them to the casserole, then pour in the wine and enough chicken stock to just cover the veal. Bring to a simmer, cover, then place in an oven preheated to 200°C/Gas Mark 6. Cook for 30 minutes, then reduce the temperature to 150°C/Gas Mark 2 and cook for 2 hours, checking every now and then. If there is no resistance when you pierce the meat with a knife, it is ready.

3 To make the gremolata, mix all the ingredients together in a bowl and set aside.

4 Remove the casserole from the oven and carefully take the veal out, then remove and discard the string. Take the meat off the bone in chunks. Use a teaspoon to extract the marrow from the bones and reserve it to add to the risotto. Discard the bones.

5 Put the casserole on the hob. Bring the liquid in the casserole to a simmer and cook until it starts to thicken slightly. This can take up to 30 minutes. If necessary, thicken the sauce with the *beurre manié* by whisking it into the sauce a small piece at a time and bringing it back to the boil. Strain the sauce through a fine sieve into a clean pan. Season well with salt, pepper and the sugar, then add the meat and heat through gently. Keep warm while you make the risotto.

6 Put the stock in a saucepan and bring to a simmer. Leave over a low heat. Add the saffron. Melt half the butter in a large sauté pan and add the onion. Cook gently until the onion is soft, then stir in the rice and cook for 1 minute, until the rice is opaque.

7 Add a ladleful of hot stock to the rice and cook, stirring constantly, until it has been absorbed. Continue adding stock in the same way, stirring continuously, and keeping it at a gentle simmer throughout. When the rice is just tender, add half the Parmesan and remove from the heat. Stir in the remaining butter, some salt and pepper and the cooked marrow from the veal, cover and leave the risotto to rest for 3 minutes.

8 Reheat the osso buco, if necessary, and stir in the gremolata. Serve the risotto in a separate dish, with the remaining Parmesan sprinkled on top.

STEAK TARTARE

Steak tartare is an absolute classic but you do need to enjoy the texture of raw meat. It's important to chop it very finely indeed, so it begins to break down slightly. Don't be tempted to put it in a food processor, though, as you still need some texture to it.

Serves 2

400g fillet of beef, trimmed

3 tablespoons very finely chopped red onion

1 tablespoon Worcestershire sauce

4 small gherkins, finely chopped

2 tablespoons capers, drained and chopped

2 tablespoons finely chopped curly parsley

a good pinch of chilli powder

3 anchovy fillets, drained, rinsed and finely chopped

juice of 1 lemon

2 eggs

sea salt and black pepper

1 Cut the beef into very small dice and put it in a bowl. Add the red onion, Worcestershire sauce, gherkin, capers, parsley, chilli powder and anchovy fillets. Mix well and season with lemon juice and salt and pepper.

2 Put a 10cm metal ring in the centre of a serving plate and press half the beef mixture into it. Remove the ring and repeat on a second plate with the remaining mixture. Separate the eggs, discarding the whites. Put the yolks back into the half-shells, and place in the centre of the beef. Serve with French bread.

ROAST SADDLE OF LAMB STUFFED WITH APRICOTS AND COUSCOUS

A whole-boned saddle of lamb looks spectacular and is a real dinner-party dish. All it needs to go with it is some Potato Wedges with Fresh Herbs and Garlic (see page 22).

Serves 8

1 boned-out whole saddle of lamb, with the skin attached

1 onion, very finely chopped

50g unsalted butter

150g button mushrooms, finely chopped

10 ready-to-eat dried apricots, quartered

50ml chicken stock

60g couscous

60g Wensleydale cheese, finely grated

grated zest of 1 lemon

3 tablespoons finely chopped curly parsley

6 thin slices of Parma ham

2 tablespoons olive oil

sea salt and black pepper

For the mint salsa verde:

15g mint leaves, chopped

2 tomatoes, deseeded and finely diced

2 garlic cloves, finely chopped

150ml extra virgin olive oil

2 tablespoons white wine vinegar

1 teaspoon fine sea salt

1 teaspoon black pepper

1 Lay the saddle of lamb, skin-side down, on a board. Pull both loins away from the skin, then carefully cut away all the remaining meat. Bash the skin with a rolling pin to make it thinner, trimming off any excess fat. Remove all the fine sinews and membrane from the loins. Place one loin across the centre of the skin and make a cut along its length, cutting halfway down to create a channel. Similarly, cut a channel along the other loin.

2 Cook the onion in the butter in a frying pan until softened. Add the mushrooms and fry for 5 minutes, until tender. Season well, then stir in the apricots.

3 Bring the chicken stock to the boil. Put the couscous in a bowl and pour over the boiling stock. Cover with cling film and leave for 20 minutes. Separate the grains with a fork, then stir in the apricot mixture, cheese, lemon zest and parsley. Season well. Squeeze the mixture together with your hands and shape it into a cylinder, slightly shorter than the loins.

4 Place a roll of cling film behind a chopping board, then pull some cling film over the board. Place the Parma ham slices lengthways on the cling film, slightly overlapping each other. Place the cylinder of couscous across the Parma ham slices at the end nearest to you. Roll up the ham to enclose the couscous mixture and make a sausage shape. Wrap tightly in the cling film and chill for 30 minutes.

5 Season the loins with salt and pepper. Remove the cling film from the Parma ham-wrapped couscous. Place it in the channel along the middle of the loin on the lamb skin. Position the other loin on top, spreading out the cut so it encases the top of the filling. Lift one side of the skin over the loins and then the other side so that they overlap by 3cm. Tie lengths of butcher's string at evenly spaced intervals around the prepared joint. Cover and leave to rest in the fridge for a few hours, or overnight.

6 Remove the lamb from the fridge 1 hour before cooking. Heat the olive oil in a large frying pan, add the saddle and cook until browned all over. Transfer to a roasting tin and place in an oven preheated to 200°C/Gas Mark 6. Cook for 25–30 minutes, depending on how you like your lamb.

7 Meanwhile, mix all the ingredients for the salsa verde together and set aside until ready to serve. Remove the lamb from the oven and leave to rest for 15 minutes before carving. Serve with the salsa verde.

HONEY-GLAZED LAMB SHANKS

The flavour you get from lamb shanks is unbeatable, thanks to the long, slow cooking they receive. You can adapt the flavours to suit wherever you are in the world — India, France, Italy. I've gone for cumin seeds here to give a piquant note, plus tomato purée for richness. The great thing about this dish is that you can cook it 3 days in advance and the flavours will only improve. Just add the glaze and finish off at the last minute.

Serves 4

4 medium lamb shanks (ask your butcher to remove the knuckle, leaving just the shank bone)

2 tablespoons olive oil

2 onions, finely chopped

4 garlic cloves, finely chopped

2 teaspoons cumin seeds

4 sprigs of thyme

2 celery sticks, chopped

1 carrot, roughly chopped

325ml red wine

1 litre chicken stock

4 bay leaves

2 large tomatoes, chopped

1 tablespoon tomato purée

Beurre Manié (see page 70, tips), made with 15g soft unsalted butter and 15g plain flour (optional)

sea salt and black pepper

For the glaze:

4 tablespoons runny honey

4 tablespoons soy sauce

1 First, trim the base of the lamb shanks so they stand up properly.

2 Heat the oil in a large flameproof casserole, add the shanks and brown them all over. Remove and set aside. Add the onions, garlic, cumin seeds, thyme, celery and carrot and cook until the vegetables are slightly browned. Pour in the red wine, bring to the boil and simmer until reduced by half.

3 Return the lamb shanks to the casserole and add the chicken stock, bay leaves, chopped tomatoes and tomato purée. Bring to a simmer, cover and place in an oven preheated to 200°C/Gas Mark 6. Cook for 30 minutes, then reduce the temperature to 150°C/Gas Mark 2 and cook for a further 2 hours or until the meat is falling off the bone.

4 Take the lamb shanks out of the casserole and set aside. Place the casserole over a medium heat, bring to the boil and simmer until the liquid has reduced by half; this can take around 45 minutes and the sauce should have a light coating consistency. Take out 4 tablespoons of liquid and reserve for the glaze. If necessary, whisk in a little *beurre manié* to thicken the remaining sauce and bring it back to the boil. Season well with salt and pepper, then strain through a fine sieve.

5 To make the glaze, mix together the honey, reserved stock and soy sauce. Put the lamb shanks on to a roasting tray and brush with the honey and soy mixture. Place in an oven preheated to 200°C/Gas Mark 6 and roast for 20 minutes, basting as often as possible, or until sticky. Remove from the oven, transfer the shanks to a warm plate and leave to rest. Reheat the sauce, pour it around the shanks and serve with Creamed Potatoes (see page 86).

MEAT

MARINATED LAMB KEBABS

This makes a lovely, spicy, lemony kebab, with the irresistible flavour of coriander seeds, which always reminds me of holidays in Greece.

Serves 4

650g leg of lamb, skin removed

1 teaspoon coarsely ground black peppercorns

2 teaspoons cumin seeds, crushed

2 garlic cloves, crushed

1 tablespoon coriander seeds, crushed

2 teaspoons coarse sea salt

2 teaspoons paprika

grated zest of 1 lemon

4 tablespoons olive oil

2 red peppers, deseeded and cut into 2cm dice

For the mint yoghurt sauce:

½ cucumber, peeled and deseeded

250ml Greek yoghurt

2 tablespoons finely chopped mint

sea salt and black pepper

1 Cut the lamb into 2cm chunks and put them into a bowl. Add all the remaining ingredients except for the red peppers. Mix well, cover and leave to marinate in the fridge overnight, or for as long as you can.

2 Cut the cucumber into small dice, then mix it with the yoghurt and mint. Season with salt and pepper, cover and set aside in the fridge.

3 Soak 4 wooden skewers in cold water for 30 minutes (this will prevent them from burning). Thread the lamb on to the skewers, alternating with the red peppers.

4 Cook under a preheated grill or on a barbecue for 10 minutes, turning regularly, until slightly charred on the outside and pink inside. Serve with the mint yoghurt sauce.

ROLLED SHOULDER OF LAMB WITH HERBS, RICE AND RAISINS

Stuffing and rolling a shoulder of lamb is quite an old-fashioned technique but its easy to do and well worth the effort. The shoulder needs longer, slower cooking than the leg to ensure it is tender. For the shoulder, I always allow 20–25 minutes per 450g, plus an extra 20 minutes.

Serves 8

2kg shoulder of lamb, boned (ask your butcher to do this)

1 large Spanish onion, sliced

2 sprigs of rosemary

sea salt and black pepper

For the stuffing:

60g unsalted butter

300g onions, finely chopped

2 large garlic cloves, finely chopped

4 rashers of streaky bacon, chopped

2 tablespoons finely chopped rosemary

4 tablespoons finely chopped curly parsley

2 tablespoons finely chopped thyme

6 rounded tablespoons cooked rice

2 tablespoons raisins, soaked in wine or water

2 tablespoons breadcrumbs

1 To make the stuffing, melt the butter in a frying pan, add the onions and cook gently until softened. Add the garlic, bacon, rosemary, parsley and thyme. Cook for 3–4 minutes, then transfer to a bowl and add the cooked rice, raisins and breadcrumbs. Season well with salt and pepper and stir to combine. Set aside to cool.

2 Unroll the lamb and season well with salt and pepper. Spread the stuffing on top and roll up the lamb, tying it tightly in several places with butcher's string. Season the lamb with salt and pepper on all sides.

3 Put the sliced onion and rosemary into a roasting tin and place the lamb on top. Place in an oven preheated to 200°C/Gas Mark 6 and roast for 30 minutes, then turn the temperature down to 160°C/Gas Mark 3 and cook for 1–1¼ hours. Insert a meat thermometer in the middle; it should register 60–65°C, giving meat that is slightly pink. Remove from the oven and allow to rest for 20 minutes, then remove the string, slice and serve.

ROAST LEG OF LAMB WITH HERBS AND LAMBS' KIDNEYS

Here the leg is boned, then stuffed with the fried kidneys and lots of fresh herbs. Serve with French beans and ratatouille. For the leg, I always allow 20 minutes per 500g, plus an extra 15 minutes or so.

Serves 6

100g unsalted butter

3 lambs' kidneys, cleaned and halved

6 tablespoons mixed chopped herbs, such as curly parsley, dill and tarragon, or 3 tablespoons dried Provençal herbs

4 garlic cloves, chopped

2.5kg leg of lamb, leg bone removed but with the knuckle left in

200ml Marsala or red wine

sea salt and black pepper

1 Melt 30g of the butter in a frying pan. Season the kidneys with salt and pepper, add them to the pan and fry until just cooked but still pink in the middle. Transfer them to a bowl, add the herbs and garlic and mix well.

2 Use the kidney mixture to stuff the leg, then tie it with kitchen string to hold it together. Rub half of the remaining butter over the lamb, then season with salt and pepper. Put 250ml water in a roasting tin and add the lamb. Place in an oven preheated to 180°C/Gas Mark 4 and roast for 1¼–1¾ hours. Insert a meat thermometer in the middle; it should register 60–65°C, giving meat that is slightly pink.

3 Remove the lamb from the oven and transfer it to a warmed serving dish. Allow to rest for 20 minutes. Meanwhile, put the roasting tin on the hob over a low-medium heat and add the Marsala or wine to enrich the sauce. Whisk in the remaining butter. Slice the lamb and and serve with kidney beans or French beans.

RAISED PIES

A raised pie is a deep pie that is traditionally moulded by hand, raising the pastry up around the filling either without support or in a special tin. For this you need a fairly stiff pastry that results in a firm crust when cooked. Classic raised pies include pork pies, game pies and veal and ham pie. Traditionally eaten cold, they are great for picnics and buffets.

There's nothing tastier than a handmade pork pie. After you master this recipe, you'll never want to buy pork pies again — homemade ones invariably taste so much better.

PORK PIES

To make the Hot Water Crust Pastry, follow steps 5 to 8
To make the jelly, follow steps 19 to 21

SERVES 2–4 PER PIE (MAKES 2 PIES)

1 tablespoon olive oil, plus a drizzle

100g onion, finely chopped

300g pork shoulder, finely chopped

300g belly pork, minced

150g pork back fat, minced

1 teaspoon ground allspice

1 teaspoon chopped sage

1 teaspoon chopped thyme

1 egg yolk

1 egg, beaten, to seal and glaze

sea salt and black pepper

FOR THE HOT WATER CRUST PASTRY:

450g plain flour, plus extra for dusting

1 teaspoon fine sea salt

160g lard, plus extra for greasing

200g water

FOR THE JELLY:

1 pig's trotter

1 onion, roughly chopped

1 carrot, peeled and roughly chopped

a few bones from the pork

a few sprigs of parsley

1 tablespoon black peppercorns

1 Heat the 1 tablespoon oil in a frying pan, add the onion and cook until softened. Transfer to a large bowl and leave to cool.

2 Add the pork and pork fat to the onion, along with the allspice, herbs and egg yolk and season with salt and pepper. Mix well.

3 Form a spoonful of the mixture into a small patty and fry it in a drizzle of oil until cooked through. Taste and adjust the seasoning if necessary.

4 Grease two 11cm loose-bottomed pork pie tins with lard.

5 To make the pastry, sift the flour and salt into a large bowl and mix well.

6 Put the lard and water into a small saucepan and bring to the boil.

7 Mix the hot liquid into the flour with a fork and then bring the mixture together with your hands to form a dough.

8 Dust a work surface with flour and knead the pastry lightly until smooth. Leave to cool slightly. Divide the pastry in half, reserving a quarter of each half for the pie lids. Cover to keep warm.

9 Roll out each large piece of pastry on a lightly floured work surface into a 28cm circle.

10 Line the prepared tins with the pastry, leaving the excess overhanging the edge.

11 Fill the pastry cases with the meat mixture up to 1cm from the top edge, packing it carefully and tightly.

12 Use a sharp knife to trim off the excess pastry around each tin.

13 Add the trimmings to the pastry reserved for the pie lids and roll into two 13cm circles.

14 Brush beaten egg around the top edge of each pastry case and sit a lid on each one.

15 To seal, press all around the edge with the flat of your fingers. Now pinch the north, south, east and west points, then pinch again in between.

16 Make a hole in the centre of the top and brush all over with beaten egg.

17 Place the pies on a hot baking tray in an oven preheated to 200°C/Gas Mark 6 and bake for 20 minutes.

18 Turn the oven down to 150°C/Gas Mark 2 and bake for another hour.

19 To make the jelly, put all the ingredients into a saucepan, cover with cold water and bring to the boil. Cook until the liquid is reduced by half.

20 Strain through a fine sieve into a clean saucepan, then reduce again to about 350ml, or enough to fill the pies.

21 Season well with salt and pepper. Leave to cool to room temperature, then pour into a jug.

22 Remove the cooked pies from the oven and leave to cool for 20 minutes.

23 Insert a funnel in the hole in the top of the pies, then carefully pour in the cooled but still liquid jelly.

24 Leave the pies to cool completely so that the jelly is set. To turn them out, place each tin on top of a ramekin and press down gently to release the pie.

pork pie variations

Pork and Apple Pies – peel, core and dice 2 apples, then sauté in a knob of unsalted butter until tender. Follow the recipe on pages 120–122, adding the sautéed apple, grated zest of 1 orange and 2 finely chopped garlic cloves to the pork mixture.

Pork and Chicken Pies – follow the recipe on pages 120–122, adding 1 skinned and boned chicken breast cut into 1–2cm dice to the pork mixture.

long pork, gammon and egg pie variations

Long Pheasant, Pork and Egg Pie – follow the recipe opposite, replacing the gammon with pheasant.

Long Chicken, Mushroom and Egg Pork Pie – follow the recipe opposite, replacing the onion with 20g sliced button mushrooms, cooked gently in the butter until soft, then drained and cooled. Add to the other filling ingredients, replacing the gammon with 400g skinned and boned chicken breasts cut into 5mm dice.

Long Wild Mushroom and Egg Pork Pie – follow the recipe opposite, replacing the onion with 400g finely chopped wild mushrooms, cooked gently in the butter until soft, being careful not to brown them. Season well with salt and pepper, then drain and leave to cool. Add to the other filling ingredients, but using only 200g diced raw gammon.

TIPS AND IDEAS

■ The reason for using hot water in the pastry for raised pies is that it makes the dough more malleable and thus easier to shape around the filling. The pastry is also firmer once cooked, which is important to keep the pie upright – a standard shortcrust would crumble.

■ The water in the recipe on page 120 is weighed in grams rather than measured in millilitres. I have got into the habit of doing this for bread and pastry since I bought electronic scales: you can simply put the bowl or pan on the scales and weigh the liquid with all the dry ingredients. If you don't have electronic scales, however, the same quantity in millilitres will be fine.

■ To ensure the pastry is pliable when you use it, make sure it is still slightly warm. Unlike other pastries, it cannot be made in advance.

■ Raised pies should be seasoned quite strongly, with plenty of salt and pepper.

■ You can mix and match the meats in a raised pie. As long as you remember to include the fat, almost any meat will do.

■ Pigs' trotters are easily obtainable from butchers and usually cost just pennies. If you don't want to bother with them, though, you can make the jelly by adding gelatine leaves to clear chicken stock – about 4 leaves to 250ml stock should do it.

■ If you have too much jelly, it can be frozen for future use. Simply defrost, then reheat gently when needed.

■ You can buy loose-bottomed raised pie tins in several sizes but springform cake tins could be used instead.

■ To make little individual pork pies, use deep muffin tins.

LONG PORK, GAMMON AND EGG PIE

This is the type of pie people think can't be made at home, but that's not the case: you don't need any special equipment, just an ordinary straight-sided loaf tin. The only thing to look out for is to make sure the eggs are neatly arranged in the centre. Serve with salad and chutneys.

Serves 8

60g unsalted butter, plus extra for greasing

100g onion, finely chopped

400g raw gammon, cut into 5mm dice

400g pork shoulder, minced

100g pork back fat, minced

3 tablespoons finely chopped curly parsley

9 coriander seeds, crushed

1 egg yolk

1 quantity of Hot Water Crust Pastry (see pages 120–121)

plain flour for dusting

5 eggs, hard-boiled and shelled

1 egg, beaten with a pinch of salt, to seal and glaze

1 quantity of Jelly (optional, see pages 120–122)

sea salt and black pepper

1 First make the filling. Melt the butter in a frying pan, add the onion and cook gently until very soft. Transfer to a large bowl and leave to cool.

2 Add the gammon, minced pork, back fat, parsley, coriander seeds and egg yolk to the onion, season well with salt and pepper and mix thoroughly.

3 Line a 26 x 10 x 7cm loaf tin with greaseproof paper buttered on both sides. Reserve one-third of the hot water crust pastry for the lid and cover to keep warm. Roll out the remaining two-thirds of the pastry on a lightly floured work surface to a rectangle about 47 x 30cm. Use to line the prepared tin, leaving the excess pastry overhanging the edges.

4 Layer one-third of the filling in the pastry case. Arrange the hard-boiled eggs along the centre, then add another third of the filling around the sides of the eggs. Top with the remaining filling.

5 Roll out the pastry for the lid, making a rectangle that will fit inside the tin. Brush around the edges on one side with the beaten egg and place, egg washed-side down, on the pie. Bring up the overhanging pastry and trim to 1cm high with scissors. Fold it over the lid, then press all around the edges with a fork. Make 2 holes in the top and brush all over with beaten egg.

6 Place the pie on a hot baking sheet in an oven preheated to 200°C/Gas Mark 6 and bake for 25 minutes. Turn the oven down to 150°C/Gas Mark 2 and bake for a further 1½ hours. Remove the pie from the oven and leave to cool for 20 minutes, then add the jelly, if using, as instructed on page 122. Leave to cool completely. Remove the pie from the tin by lifting it out with the greaseproof paper.

RAISED GAME PIE

This is the perfect Christmas treat and is so useful if you've got a lot of people coming to visit. You can make it look very pretty by cutting shapes out of the pastry trimmings to decorate the top. In the past, a lighter pastry was made especially for elaborate decorations.

Serves 12

60g unsalted butter

100g onion, finely chopped

2 tablespoons juniper berries, crushed

2 garlic cloves, crushed

2 teaspoons Chinese five-spice powder

900g belly pork or pork shoulder, minced

150g button mushrooms, sliced

900g venison, 400g pheasant and 200g rabbit meat, or 1.6kg mixture of game meat, cut into chunks

4 tablespoons port (optional)

1 egg yolk

sea salt and black pepper

For the hot water crust pastry:

900g plain flour, plus extra for dusting

2 teaspoons fine sea salt

100g unsalted butter, plus extra for greasing

100g lard

250g water

1 egg yolk, beaten, to seal and glaze

1 First make the filling. Melt half the butter in a frying pan, add the onion and cook gently until very soft. Add the juniper berries, garlic and five-spice powder and leave to cool. Put into a large bowl with the minced pork, season well with salt and pepper and mix thoroughly.

2 Melt the remaining 30g butter in the frying pan, add the mushrooms and cook until soft. Drain and leave to cool.

3 Put the game meat into a separate bowl, add the port, if using, the egg yolk and cooled mushrooms and season well with salt and pepper. Mix well.

4 Butter a 26cm loose-bottomed cake tin. Make the hot water crust pastry as instructed on page 121, steps 5–7, adding the butter to the lard with the water before bringing to the boil. After kneading, reserve one-third of the pastry for the lid and cover to keep warm. Roll out the remaining two-thirds of the pastry on a lightly floured work surface and use to line the prepared tin, leaving the excess pastry overhanging the edge.

5 Layer one-third of the pork mixture in the pastry case, cover with half the game mixture, then add another third of the pork. Top with the remaining game mixture and add a final layer of pork.

6 Roll out the pastry for the lid making it just large enough to rest on the edges of the tin. Brush the beaten egg around the top edge of the pastry case and sit the lid on it. Bring up the overhanging pastry and trim to 1cm high with scissors. Fold it over the lid, then press all around the edge with the flat of your fingers to seal. Now pinch the pastry together, as on page 122, step 15. Make 1 or 2 holes in the top and brush all over with beaten egg. Roll out the pastry trimmings, cut out shapes, such as leaves and flowers, and use to decorate the top of the pie. To prevent the pastry from over-browning, wrap a doubled piece of brown paper around the pie and secure with string.

7 Place the pie on a hot baking sheet in an oven preheated to 200°C/Gas Mark 6 and bake for 15 minutes. Turn the oven down to 150°C/Gas Mark 2 and bake for a further 2 hours. Remove the pie from the oven and leave to cool completely before removing from the tin.

CHICKEN, HAM, TARRAGON AND POTATO PIE

My family always ask me to cook this when they come to stay. Although it's not a traditional raised pie, and uses puff pastry rather than hot water crust, I have included it in this chapter because it is a sturdy pie that is completely enclosed in the pastry.

Serves 6

130g unsalted butter

800g all-purpose potatoes, such as Maris Piper, peeled and very thinly sliced with a mandoline

300g thickly sliced cooked ham, cut into 5mm dice

4 tablespoons chopped tarragon or 1 tablespoon dried tarragon

2 large chicken breasts, skinned and boned and cut into thin strips

1 egg yolk,

500g puff pastry

plain flour for dusting

1 egg, beaten, to seal and glaze

200ml double cream

sea salt and black pepper

1 Melt 100g of the butter in a large frying pan, add the potatoes and cook over a medium heat without browning until they are tender – this will take 30–40 minutes. Transfer to a dish. Add the ham and tarragon, season well with salt and pepper and mix thoroughly.

2 Melt the remaining 30g butter in the pan, add the chicken strips and heat gently until just cooked through. Leave to rest for 10 minutes, until the juices run out, then add, along with the egg yolk, to the potato mixture. Season generously with salt and pepper, then mix well and leave to cool completely.

3 Roll out one-third of the pastry on a lightly floured work surface into a 30cm circle. Roll the remaining two-thirds of the pastry into a 38cm circle. Lay the smaller pastry circle on a baking sheet, pile the potato mixture in the centre and brush the beaten egg all around the outside edge. Place the larger pastry circle on top and press down around the filling to seal and form a hat shape. Trim around the edge to leave a 5cm border of pastry. Brush the border with beaten egg, then gently fold it inwards and crimp firmly all the way around. Cut an 8cm circle in the top, but leave the lid in place, then brush the pie all over with beaten egg. Place in an oven preheated to 200°C/ Gas Mark 6 and bake for 25 minutes. Turn the oven down to 150°C/Gas Mark 2 and bake for a further 30 minutes, rotating the baking sheet if the pie is cooking faster on one side than the other.

4 Remove the pie from the oven. Bring the cream to the boil in a saucepan. Lift the little pastry lid with a sharp knife and pour the cream into the pie, making sure it spreads to the edge of the filling inside. Close the lid and return to the oven for another 15–20 minutes. Transfer to a dish to serve.

CURING

Curing is an ancient form of preserving in which the food is either put in a liquid brine (wet curing) or simply covered in a mixture of salt and spices or other flavourings (dry curing). In the days before refrigeration, it was vital to preserve food in this way. It's still well worth doing for the delicious flavours it creates and for its tenderising effect. Although preparing a cure doesn't take much time, in most cases you will have to wait before you can enjoy your cured meat or fish — sometimes for several weeks.

In this recipe, fresh pork is wet cured to transform it into gammon, and once it is cooked it becomes ham. Curing a whole leg of pork is for real enthusiasts — you have to plan it a good month in advance and be sure to have the right equipment.

WHOLE LEG OF GLAZED CURED HAM

To cure the leg of pork, follow steps 1 to 18
To glaze the ham, follow steps 19 to 22

SERVES 20

1 leg of pork, weighing about 6kg

500g sea salt

2 onions, roughly chopped

2 carrots, peeled and roughly chopped

4 celery sticks, roughly chopped

4 bay leaves

3 star anise pods

1 tablespoon black peppercorns

1 tablespoon coriander seeds

a few sprigs of parsley

FOR THE BRINE:

18 litres water

3kg fine sea salt, plus an extra 500g if needed

3kg granulated sugar

10 bay leaves

6 tablespoons black peppercorns, crushed

4 tablespoons allspice berries, crushed

2 tablespoons saltpetre (optional)

FOR THE GLAZE:

about 100 cloves

350g soft dark brown sugar

200ml thick runny honey

1 tablespoon Dijon mustard

1 Fill a large, non-metallic container with boiling water to sterilise it, then pour it out and leave the container to cool.

2 Place the pork on a board and rub the salt into every crevice of the meat.

3 Place the pork in the sterilised container and cover with a board.

4 Place weights, such as large food cans, on top of the board. Leave in a cool place for at least 12 hours to draw out the liquid from the meat.

5 To make the brine, put the water, salt, sugar, bay leaves and spices and saltpetre, if using, into a very large saucepan and bring to the boil.

6 Reduce the heat and simmer for 2 minutes. Turn off the heat and leave until completely cold.

7 Drain the liquid from the pork, then cover it with the cold brine. Cover and leave in a cool place for a month.

8 Test the salt level every week by adding an egg or a potato to the brine – if it sinks halfway rather than floating, you need to add more salt.

9 To do this, ladle about 250ml of the brine into a saucepan and add the extra 500g salt to it.

10 Bring to the boil, then leave to cool completely. Add to the remaining brine and test again as in step 8.

11 When the month is up, pour off the brine and wash the pork well under cold running water.

12 Put the pork into a very large saucepan, cover it with cold water and leave to soak overnight.

13 Pour off the soaking water, cover with fresh cold water and bring to the boil. Reduce the heat and simmer for 15 minutes.

14 Pour off the water, cover with fresh cold water, bring to the boil, then simmer for another 15 minutes. If the water is still salty, repeat once more.

15 When the water is no longer salty, pour it away and cover the pork with fresh cold water. Add the onions, carrots, celery, bay leaves, spices and parsley.

16 Bring up to a very gentle simmer and cook for about 4 hours (20 minutes per 500g), until the rind pulls away easily, checking after 3½ hours.

17 Check the internal temperature of the ham by inserting a meat thermometer – it should register at least 75°C.

18 When the ham is fully cooked, remove from the pan and transfer to a roasting tin.

19 To glaze the ham, remove all the rind while the ham is still warm, leaving as much fat on as possible. Leave to rest for 1 hour.

20 Using a sharp knife, score the fat into a diamond pattern by cutting long diagonal lines first one way and then the other.

21 Insert a clove into each corner of the diamonds.

22 Combine the sugar, honey and mustard and use a pastry brush to spread the mixture all over the ham.

23 Place the ham in an oven preheated to 180°C/Gas Mark 4.

24 Bake for about 25 minutes, or until the fat is caramelised, basting every 10 minutes to achieve a good colour. Serve with Cumberland sauce.

glazed cured ham variations

Glazed Ham with Ginger – follow the recipe on pages 130–132, but purée 4 pieces of stem ginger in a food processor with a little of the ginger syrup and use in the glaze instead of honey.

Cider-cured Ham – follow the recipe on pages 130–132, using cider instead of water in the brine. You could also try varying the flavourings: sage or star anise would be lovely.

Double-glazed ham – for a really rich finish, glaze the ham as described on page 132, let it cool, then repeat the glaze and return the ham to the oven for 20 minutes.

TIPS AND IDEAS

■ Make sure you have a large enough container and that all your utensils are sterilised with boiling water and your work surfaces are very clean.

■ The trick with brining is to ensure that the salt penetrates all the way through, so the ham keeps well and no bacteria can be introduced. This is why I rub salt into the crevices before brining, to give the meat a quick dry-cure and make doubly sure.

■ If you like, you could pierce the meat with a skewer 3 or 4 times before putting it in the brine, to help it penetrate.

■ Saltpetre (potassium nitrate) keeps the meat a nice pink colour and also helps preserve it. It's now readily available online but do leave it out if you can't get it or prefer not to use it.

■ As you need to leave the meat in a cool place while it is curing, this is probably not something to make in the summer months. A cool larder is ideal, or an outhouse or garage – as long as you cover the container tightly to prevent pests and other intruders getting at the contents.

■ If you prefer to cure a smaller joint of pork, halve the quantities of the curing mixture and reduce the curing time to 2 weeks. Cook for 25 minutes per 500g.

■ Instead of Cumberland sauce, you could serve the ham with parsley sauce or, at Christmas, with cranberry and orange sauce.

■ The ham will keep for a week or so in the fridge. It also freezes well.

HOME-CURED HAM QUICHE

This is an ideal way to use up the leftovers from your lovely home-cured ham, but of course any good-quality ham will do. Season the egg mixture carefully because the ham may be quite salty.

Serves 6–8

15g unsalted butter

1 tablespoon olive oil

1 onion, finely chopped

2 eggs

2 egg yolks

100g Cheddar cheese, finely grated

350ml double cream (or half whipping and half double cream)

250g cooked ham, finely diced

sea salt and black pepper

For the shortcrust pastry:

250g plain flour, plus extra for dusting

½ teaspoon salt

125g cold unsalted butter, cut into small cubes

2 egg yolks

3–4 tablespoons cold water

1 First make the pastry. Sift the flour and salt into a large bowl. Add the cubed butter and rub it into the flour with your fingertips until the mixture resembles fine breadcrumbs. Make a well in the centre. Mix the egg yolks in a small bowl with 3 tablespoons of the cold water. Pour this liquid into the centre of the flour mixture. Stir with a round-bladed knife or a fork to bring everything together into a fairly firm, smooth dough. If it's too dry, add the remaining tablespoon of water. Knead lightly for a few seconds, then shape the dough into a cylinder, wrap in cling film and leave in the fridge for at least 30 minutes.

2 Roll the pastry out on a lightly floured work surface into a large circle about 3mm thick. Use it to line a 23cm loose-bottomed tart tin, about 4cm deep: carefully fold the pastry circle into 4, making a triangle. Put the point in the centre of the tin, then unfold the pastry. Take a walnut-sized ball of the excess pastry, wrap it in cling film and use it to press the pastry circle well into the sides of the tin. Leave the pastry hanging over the edge, then run the rolling pin lightly over the tin to remove the excess. Using your thumbs, press the pastry gently up the side of the tin so that it comes about 5mm above the top. Leave in the fridge for 30 minutes.

3 Prick the base of the chilled pastry case with a fork. Take a large piece of baking parchment and scrunch it up, then unfold it and use to line the pastry case. Fill it with baking beans, rice or ordinary dried beans – you can keep them and re-use them endlessly.

4 Place the tin on a hot baking sheet in an oven preheated to 200°C/Gas Mark 6 and bake for 15–20 minutes, then remove the paper and beans or rice and return the pastry case to the oven for 5 minutes, until the base is lightly coloured. Set aside while you make the filling. Leave the oven on.

5 Melt the butter with the oil in a frying pan. Add the onion and cook gently until softened, but don't let it brown. Set aside to cool. Lightly whisk together the eggs, egg yolks, Cheddar and cream and season well with salt and pepper. Put the onion and the ham into the pastry case. Pour in the egg mixture. Put the quiche straight into the oven and cook for 15 minutes. Turn the oven down to 150°C/Gas Mark 2 and cook for a further 10–15 minutes, until pale golden brown. Leave to cool slightly before serving.

HOME-CURED BRESAOLA SALAD WITH ROCKET AND SPICED MORELLO CHERRIES

Bresaola is an Italian dish of beef cured in red wine — a great way to use the wet-curing technique. The spiced Morello cherries go so well with the beef and are made with storecupboard ingredients — simplicity itself.

Serves 12 as a starter, 6 as a main course

For the bresaola:

1½ bottles of red wine

600g coarse sea salt

400g soft brown sugar

1 teaspoon saltpetre (optional)

1 tablespoon crushed peppercorns

1 tablespoon juniper berries

6 red chillies, chopped

1 cinnamon stick

a few sprigs of thyme

1.8kg piece of beef topside, the same width throughout

For the spiced Morello cherries:

750g Morello cherries from a jar

300g caster sugar

100ml port or water

a generous squeeze of lemon juice

3 cinnamon sticks

For the vinaigrette:

1 tablespoon Dijon mustard

2 tablespoons white wine vinegar

150ml extra virgin olive oil

150ml walnut oil

150ml sunflower oil

1½ teaspoons caster sugar

fine sea salt and black pepper

For the rocket salad:

6 handfuls of small-leaf wild rocket

18 large radishes, thinly sliced

1½ red onions, very thinly sliced

1 First make the brine for the bresaola. Put the wine, salt, sugar, saltpetre, if using, spices and thyme into a large saucepan and bring to the boil. Turn off the heat and leave to cool completely.

2 Fill a large, non-metallic container with boiling water to sterilise it, then pour it out and leave the container to cool. Put the beef into the sterilised container, then pour over the cold brine. Cover and leave in the fridge for 4–5 days, turning the beef every day. Pour off the brine, wipe the beef clean and dry it well. Wrap in a single layer of muslin so that it can breathe, and hang in a cool, dry place for 3–4 weeks.

3 To prepare the spiced Morello cherries, put all the ingredients into a small saucepan and heat until simmering. Simmer until the liquid is reduced to a syrup, then set aside to cool. Remove the cinnamon sticks before serving.

4 For the vinaigrette, put the mustard and vinegar into a small bowl and whisk until combined. Gradually pour in the 3 oils, whisking all the time. Add the sugar, then season with salt and pepper to taste.

5 To prepare the salad, put all the ingredients into a bowl, season with salt and pepper and add 2 tablespoons of dressing. Toss when ready to serve.

6 Slice the beef very thinly, then cut into strips. Toss the salad and place on serving plates with the beef arranged on top. Dot a few cherries around the plates and drizzle with a little of the cherry syrup.

HOME-CURED SALT BEEF COOKED IN RED WINE

It's well worth curing salt beef yourself. The flavours are much more intense than you will find in commercially cured beef. The meat is cured for a relatively short time here and then cooked in red wine until meltingly tender. Serve as part of a buffet, or as a starter with Celeriac Remoulade (see page 25).

Serves 8–10

2.5kg piece of beef brisket or topside

For the brine:

4 litres water

600g coarse sea salt

250g soft brown sugar

2 teaspoons saltpetre (optional)

2 teaspoons crushed black peppercorns

2 teaspoons crushed coriander seeds

2 teaspoons crushed allspice berries

2 bay leaves

For cooking the beef:

2 carrots, peeled and chopped

1 onion, chopped

1 garlic bulb

a few sprigs of parsley

red wine, to cover

1 First put all the ingredients for the brine into a large saucepan and bring to the boil. Turn off the heat and leave to cool completely.

2 Fill a large, non-metallic container with boiling water to sterilise it, then pour it out and leave the container to cool. Put the beef into the sterilised container and pour over the cold brine. Cover and leave in the fridge for 4–5 days, turning the beef every day.

3 Remove from the fridge, pour off the brine and wash the beef under cold running water.

4 Put the beef into a large saucepan and cover with cold water. Bring to the boil, then reduce the heat and simmer for 10 minutes. Pour off the water, add the carrots, onion, garlic bulb and parsley and cover with red wine. Bring to a simmer, then partially cover with a lid and continue simmering for about 2–2½ hours or until very tender and a fork inserted into the meat comes out easily. Transfer the beef to a board and leave to cool completely.

SALT BEEF WITH LATKES

This recipe takes me back to when I first married. My father-in-law was Jewish and I discovered the joys of salt beef with latkes (potato pancakes), which he adored.

Serves 8–10

1 quantity of Home-cured Salt Beef (see opposite, steps 1–3), using brisket

6 carrots, peeled and chopped

2 onions, chopped

1 celery stick, chopped

1 tablespoon black peppercorns

2 sprigs of thyme

2 sprigs of parsley

3 bay leaves

4 small onions, peeled but left whole

4 small turnips, peeled but left whole

1 celery heart, cut in half

8 garlic cloves, peeled but left whole

sprigs of flat-leaf parsley, to garnish

For the latkes:

500g all-purpose potatoes, such as Maris Piper

25g plain flour

1 egg yolk

a knob of butter, plus extra if needed

2 tablespoons olive oil, plus extra if needed

sea salt and black pepper

1 Put the salt beef into a large saucepan and cover with cold water. Bring to the boil, then reduce the heat and simmer for 10 minutes. Pour off the water, add 2 of the carrots, the 2 onions, celery stick, peppercorns and herbs and cover with fresh cold water. Bring to a simmer, then partially cover with a lid and continue simmering for about 2 hours. Remove the vegetables, replace with the remaining 4 carrots, the small onions, turnips, celery heart and garlic cloves and cook the beef for a further 30 minutes, until very tender and a fork inserted into the meat comes out easily.

2 Meanwhile, make the latkes. Peel the potatoes, then grate finely. Place on a clean tea towel and squeeze out as much liquid as possible. Put the potato into a bowl, add the flour and egg yolk and season well with salt and pepper. Melt the butter with the oil in a large frying pan over a medium heat. Take a handful of the potato mixture, form into a patty about 1cm thick and add to the pan. Repeat with the remaining potato mixture until the pan is full. Cook over a medium-high heat for 5 minutes, then carefully turn the latkes over and cook for a further 5 minutes. Remove from the pan and keep warm. Repeat with the remaining potato mixture, adding more butter and oil to the pan as needed.

3 Remove the salt beef and vegetables from the saucepan and serve with the latkes, garnished with sprigs of flat-leaf parsley.

SALT BEEF WITH WALNUT AND OLIVE SALAD

This refreshing winter salad is an excellent way to use up leftover salt beef.

Serves 4

500g Home-cured Salt Beef Cooked in Red Wine (see page 138)

1 head of chicory, thinly sliced crossways

100g baby red chard or mixed baby leaves

100g beansprouts

6 mint leaves, finely chopped

12 walnuts, shelled

12 stoned black olives, halved

sea salt and black pepper

For the dressing:

3 teaspoons mustard

2 limes, segmented (see page 41, step 27)

juice of 1 orange

1 tablespoon honey

50ml extra virgin olive oil

sea salt and black pepper

1 Cut the beef into slices 2–3mm thick. Set aside.

2 Combine the chicory with all the other salad ingredients in a large bowl and season well with salt and pepper.

3 Put all the dressing ingredients in a blender and blitz to a purée. Toss with the salad and serve with the salt beef.

SALT BEEF ON RYE WITH MUSTARD

There's nothing better than a sandwich made with warm salt beef. It is absolutely delicious.

Serves 4

700g Home-cured Salt Beef Cooked in Red Wine (see page 138)

To serve:

unsalted butter, for spreading

8 slices of rye bread

English mustard

wild rocket

red onion, thinly sliced into rings

pickled cucumber, sliced

1 Cut the salt beef into slices. Set aside.

2 To make the sandwiches, butter slices of rye bread, smear them with mustard, add some slices of salt beef, then top with wild rocket, red onion rings and pickled cucumber slices and finish with another slice of buttered rye bread.

This is an example of dry curing, in which you cover the food in salt to draw out the moisture. It then firms up and, with the moisture removed, will keep for longer. Nothing could be simpler. I am on a mission to persuade everyone to make gravadlax. It is far more interesting to eat than smoked salmon, and you can make so many variations on the classic recipe.

GRAVADLAX

with dill mayonnaise

To marinate the salmon, follow steps 1 to 9

SERVES AT LEAST 8

1 salmon, weighing about 2–2.5kg, cleaned, scaled (see page 173, tips) and filleted (see page 169, steps 1–3), or ask your fishmonger to do this for you; total prepared weight is about 1.5kg

FOR THE DRY CURE:

300g granulated sugar

200g coarse sea salt

4 tablespoons chopped dill, plus 4 rounded tablespoons

2 teaspoons white peppercorns, crushed

grated zest of 2 lemons and 2 limes

FOR THE DILL MAYONNAISE:

2 egg yolks

2 tablespoons Dijon mustard

250ml sunflower oil

juice of 1 lemon

2 teaspoons caster sugar

1 rounded tablespoon finely chopped dill

fine sea salt and black pepper

1 First make the dry cure. Mix the sugar, salt, 4 tablespoons dill, the crushed peppercorns and citrus zests together in a bowl.

2 Gently rub each fillet with your finger to find any remaining bones and remove them with tweezers.

3 Lay one fillet, skin-side down, on a large, doubled sheet of foil.

4 Spread the curing mixture over it, then place the other fillet on top, flesh-side down.

5 Wrap the fish up, place in a tray and leave in the fridge for 2 days and nights, turning the parcel every 8 hours and pouring away the liquid that leaks out.

6 Open the parcel, separate the fillets and scrape off the curing mixture.

7 Don't be tempted to wash the flesh side, but do rinse the skin side. Pat dry with a clean cloth.

8 Sprinkle the remaining 4 rounded tablespoons dill all over the flesh side of the fish and pat down.

9 If not using straight away, sandwich the fillets together again, wrap in cling film and store in the fridge for up to 5 days.

10 To make the dill mayonnaise, whisk together the egg yolks and 1 tablespoon of the mustard, then slowly whisk in the oil drop by drop, until it starts to thicken.

11 Pour in the remaining oil in a slow, steady stream, then whisk in the lemon juice, sugar, dill and the remaining mustard. Season with salt and pepper.

12 Unwrap the gravadlax. Starting at the tail end, slice thinly on the diagonal. Serve with the dill mayonnaise and toast.

143

TIPS AND IDEAS

■ Fish for curing must be absolutely fresh. Order it in advance from a good fishmonger and tell them what you plan to do with it.

■ It's very important to remove all the pin bones from the salmon. Run your fingers carefully over each fillet to check, and then use tweezers to pull out the bones.

■ The purpose of the dry cure is simply to remove liquid from the flesh, but it can also be a means of adding flavour. It's worth a little experimentation here – cardamom and coriander would work well, as would fennel seeds.

■ It's very important to turn the fish over, as described in step 5, so that it cures evenly.

■ If you want to do a quicker version of gravadlax, put the fillets side by side in a dish, prick them all over with a fork and sprinkle the curing mixture over them. Cover and leave in the fridge overnight, then pour away the liquid as described in step 5.

■ Gravadlax can be stored in the fridge for up to 5 days, and also freezes well. It is very useful to have ready at times like Christmas and Easter, when you have family to stay, and it is so much cheaper to make than to buy.

gravadlax variations

Beetroot Gravadlax – follow the recipe on pages 142–143 but for the curing mixture mix together 500g peeled and coarsely grated raw beetroot, 350g granulated sugar, 200g coarse sea salt, 6 tablespoons chopped dill, 2 tablespoons juniper berries and the grated zest of 2 lemons.

Mustard, Smoked Garlic and Lemon Gravadlax – follow the recipe on pages 142–143 but for the curing mixture mix together 200g coarse sea salt, 125g each granulated sugar and soft light brown sugar, the grated zest of 1 lemon, 2 tablespoons crushed yellow mustard seeds and 2 very finely chopped smoked garlic cloves.

Swordfish or Trout Gravadlax – follow the recipe on pages 142–143, substituting swordfish or trout for the salmon.

CURED SWEET BEEF

This is very similar to salt beef (see page 138) but made with a dry cure rather than a brine. To get all the lovely flavours of the curing mixture into the meat, it's important to rub it in really well. The beef is wonderful served with a salad of rocket or watercress and finely sliced pear. Here it's cooked in beer or water but you could also cook it in red wine.

Serves 20

2.5kg piece of beef brisket or topside

For the dry cure:

200g soft brown sugar

150g coarse sea salt

2 teaspoons saltpetre (optional)

2 tablespoons black peppercorns, crushed

1 tablespoon coriander seeds, crushed

1 teaspoon allspice berries, crushed

3 cloves, crushed

For cooking the beef:

2 carrots, peeled and chopped

1 onion, chopped

1 garlic bulb

a few sprigs of parsley

beer or water, to cover

1 First cure the beef. Fill a large, non-metallic container with boiling water to sterilise it, then pour it out and leave the container to cool. Put the beef into the sterilised container. Combine all the ingredients for the cure, then rub the mixture all over the meat. Cover and leave in the fridge for a minimum of 3 days, but preferably 8 days, rubbing in the curing mixture every day.

2 Remove the beef from the fridge and wash off the curing mixture under cold running water. Put the beef into a large saucepan and cover with cold water. Bring to the boil, then reduce the heat and simmer for 10 minutes. Pour off the water, add the carrots, onion, garlic bulb and parsley and cover with beer or fresh cold water. Bring to a simmer and continue simmering for about 2½ hours, until very tender, or a fork inserted into the meat comes out easily. Transfer the beef to a board and leave to cool completely.

3 To serve, carve the beef into wafer-thin slices (or ask your butcher to carve it very thinly for you) and accompany with Celeriac Remoulade (see page 25).

HOME-CURED OX TONGUE TERRINE

For anyone who loves tongue, this recipe is a dream. It smells divine while it is curing.
I got the idea from a very old recipe book, but I mellowed the flavour slightly by replacing
some of the black treacle with golden syrup.

Serves 14

2 ox tongues

2 gelatine leaves

For the dry cure:

1kg sea salt flakes

600g black treacle

200g golden syrup

2 tablespoons allspice berries, crushed

1 teaspoon saltpetre (optional)

For cooking the tongues:

1 large onion, chopped

2 carrots, peeled and chopped

1 tablespoon black peppercorns

a few sprigs of thyme

1 bay leaf

1 First cure the tongues. Take a bowl just large enough to hold the tongues and fill it with boiling water to sterilise it. Pour out the water and leave the bowl to cool. Pierce the tongues all over with a skewer, then put them into the sterilised bowl. Mix all the cure ingredients together, then rub all over the tongues. Cover and leave in the fridge for 3 weeks, turning every day.

2 Remove from the fridge and wash off all the curing mixture under cold running water. Put the tongues into a large saucepan and cover with cold water. Add the onion, carrots, peppercorns, thyme and bay leaf and bring to a simmer. Continue simmering for about 3½ hours, or until the skin of the tongues comes away.

3 Remove the tongues from the pan and leave until cool enough to handle, then peel off the skin. Remove any small bones from the neck end of the tongues.

4 Soften the gelatine leaves in 100ml of the hot cooking liquid from the tongue saucepan. Pour a little of the gelatine into a 26 x 10 x 7cm terrine dish or loaf tin. Add the tongues while they are still warm, then add the remaining gelatine. Cover the dish or tin with a sheet of greaseproof paper and place weights on top, such as some food cans. Leave in a cool place for at least 24 hours before turning out and slicing.

OX TONGUE WITH PEAR, CELERIAC AND DILL AND PARSLEY PESTO

Although this might seem an unlikely combination of flavours, it is absolutely wonderful. The pears marry beautifully with the tongue, but plums work equally well.

Serves 4

350g celeriac, peeled (200g prepared weight)

2 pears, peeled, cored and finely diced

2 teaspoons lemon juice

1 tablespoon small capers

3 tablespoons mayonnaise

2 tablespoons finely chopped chives

½ teaspoon Dijon mustard

1 quantity of Home-cured Ox Tongue Terrine (see page 147)

sea salt and black pepper

For the dill and parsley pesto:

2 tablespoons chopped dill

2 tablespoons chopped flat-leaf parsley

½ garlic clove, peeled

1 teaspoon coarse sea salt

6 tablespoons olive oil

1 Cut the celeriac into very fine strips. Place in a bowl with the pears, lemon juice and capers and mix well. Add the mayonnaise, chives and mustard and mix again. Season well with salt and pepper and set aside until ready to serve.

2 To make the pesto, put the herbs, garlic and salt into a small food processor and whiz together, then add the oil, season with pepper and process again. The pesto should have a sauce consistency, so if necessary add a little water to loosen it.

3 To serve, place 3 slices of tongue on each serving plate with a small pile of the pear celeriac on the side and a drizzle of the pesto.

CURED CHICKEN WITH LEMON

A great alternative to roast chicken, this involves a relatively quick cure of just 1–2 days. By drawing some of the liquid out of the bird, you concentrate the flavours. The lemon juice, brown sugar and honey give a delightful sweet and sour taste.

Serves 4

3 tablespoons soft brown sugar

2 tablespoons clear honey

1 chicken, weighing about 1.5kg

1½ tablespoons coarse sea salt

1 teaspoon black peppercorns, crushed

juice and grated zest of 2 lemons

olive oil for drizzling

1 First rub the sugar and honey into the chicken, then rub in the salt and pepper and finally the lemon juice and zest. Put the chicken into a bowl, cover and leave in the fridge for 1–2 days, turning it about every 4 hours or whenever you can.

2 Remove from the fridge, pour off any liquid and transfer directly to a roasting tin. Drizzle with olive oil, place in an oven preheated to 150°C/ Gas Mark 2 and roast for about 1¼ hours or until the juices run clear when a knife is inserted into the thickest part of the thigh, near the bone. If the chicken is browning too quickly, cover with a sheet of foil and continue roasting.

3 Remove the bird from the oven and leave to rest for 20 minutes before carving. Serve with sautéed potatoes.

CURED DUCK BREAST WITH HERB SALAD AND WALNUT VINAIGRETTE

This is based on a recipe in my book Castle Cook and remains one of my favourites. I hang the duck breasts in the garage to dry, but any cool, dry place will do. It's important not to overwrap them or they won't dry properly.

Serves 4 as a first course

2 boned Barbary duck breasts, weighing about 360g each

For the dry cure:

40g coarse sea salt

5 juniper berries, crushed

5 black peppercorns, crushed

5 allspice berries, crushed

1 bay leaf

zest of 1 orange, cut into fine strips

For the walnut vinaigrette:

4 garlic cloves, crushed

6 tablespoons extra virgin olive oil

3 tablespoons walnut oil

juice of ½ lemon

fine sea salt and black pepper

For the herb salad:

a handful of rocket

a handful of chervil

a handful of coriander

a handful of flat-leaf parsley

a few tarragon leaves

1 First cure the duck. Mix all the cure ingredients together. Lay the duck breasts, skin-side down, in a dish and cover with the curing mixture. Cover and leave in the fridge for 36 hours.

2 Scrape off all the curing mixture, then roll each breast into a sausage shape. Wrap each roll in muslin and secure firmly at each end with butcher's string, and then at 2cm intervals along its length.

3 Hang the wrapped duck breasts in a cool, dry place for 2–3 weeks. They are ready when they are firm to touch. Store them in the fridge until you are ready to serve them.

4 For the dressing, mix all the ingredients together in a bowl and leave to infuse for 4 hours. Strain the mixture into a jug.

5 To prepare the salad, remove the stalks from the herbs, then carefully rinse the leaves under cold running water and shake dry in a clean tea towel. Toss them with 1 tablespoon of the dressing – serve the rest separately, or reserve it for another occasion.

6 Unwrap the duck breasts and slice extremely thinly. Serve with the herb salad.

SALT COD BRANDADE WITH POACHED EGG

Salt cod is popular in the Mediterranean, where it is dried out completely, then rehydrated in water before use. In this version it is salted for just 24 hours, which has the effect of drawing out some of the moisture and firming up the flesh slightly.

Serves 4

coarse sea salt for encasing the cod

550g cod fillet

1 teaspoon white wine vinegar

4 eggs

2 bay leaves

150g potatoes, peeled and cut into 2cm pieces

300ml double cream

½ teaspoon freshly grated nutmeg

50ml olive oil

1 garlic clove, finely chopped

4 tablespoons finely chopped chives

4 ripe tomatoes

black pepper

sprigs of chervil, to garnish

1 First prepare the salt cod. Spread a layer of salt over the base of a gratin dish. Lay the cod on top and cover with another layer of salt. Cover the dish and leave in the fridge overnight.

2 Meanwhile, prepare the poached eggs in advance. Fill a saucepan three-quarters full with water and add the vinegar. Bring to the boil, then reduce the heat to a simmer. Crack an egg into a small bowl. Draw a long-handled spoon through the water in a circular motion to create a vortex. Slide the egg into the water and continue stirring around it once or twice so that the white attaches itself to the yolk. Repeat with another egg. Cook each egg for 2½ minutes, then check for doneness: lift the egg out with a slotted spoon and gently press the white to make sure it's cooked through. If ready, transfer immediately to a bowl of iced water. Cook the remaining 2 eggs in the same way and add to the iced water. Leave them in the fridge until ready to serve (they will keep for up to 2 days as long as you change the water every day).

3 Remove the cod from the fridge, wash off all the salt under cold running water and dry well. Put the cod into a saucepan of cold water with the bay leaves and bring to a simmer, then simmer gently for about 8 minutes, until just cooked. Drain the cod well, then flake into a bowl, discarding the skin and any bones.

4 Cook the potatoes in a saucepan of boiling water until tender. Drain well and return to the pan. Bring the cream to the boil in a separate saucepan, then reduce the heat and simmer for a few minutes. Turn off the heat and leave to cool slightly. Put the cod into a food processor with the nutmeg and lightly pulse together, pouring in half the cream as you do so. The mixture needs to retain some texture.

5 Add the oil to the potatoes and mash them, then beat in the remaining cream. Season with pepper. Fold in the cod mixture, garlic and chives. Keep warm.

6 To reheat the poached eggs, put into saucepan of simmering water for 40 seconds.

7 To serve, slice one tomato into rounds and make a spiral on a serving plate. Pack one-quarter of the brandade mixture into a metal ring or pastry cutter and arrange on top of the tomato. Top with a poached egg and garnish with sprigs of chervil. Repeat with the remaining tomatoes, cod mixture and poached eggs.

SALT COD FISH CAKES

This is another wonderful way of using salt cod, and a great twist on conventional fish cakes.

Serves 6

500g floury potatoes, peeled and cut into equal-sized chunks

450g Salt Cod (see page 151, steps 1 and 3)

10g soft unsalted butter

2 tablespoons finely chopped chives

2 tablespoons finely chopped parsley

grated zest of 1 lemon

a pinch of cayenne pepper

100g plain flour

3 eggs, lightly beaten

200g fresh fine white breadcrumbs

sunflower oil for deep-frying

white pepper

lemon wedges, to serve

1 Cook the potatoes in a large saucepan of boiling water until tender. Drain well, return to the pan and mash. Transfer to a large bowl.

2 Put the salt cod and butter into a food processor and process until smooth. Add to the potato with the herbs, lemon zest and cayenne, season with white pepper and mix well. Shape the mixture into patties 5cm round and 2cm thick, cover and leave in the fridge for 4 hours.

3 Put the flour into a shallow bowl, the beaten eggs into a separate bowl and the breadcrumbs into another bowl. Turn each fish cake in the flour, then dip into the beaten eggs and finally roll in the breadcrumbs to coat.

4 Heat some sunflower oil in a deep-fat fryer or a large, deep saucepan to 170°C. Fry the fish cakes in batches for about 5 minutes, until golden. Drain on kitchen paper and serve with lemon wedges.

CURED MACKEREL

This makes one of the best and simplest first courses ever. Mackerel is hugely underrated and great value – but remember, the fresher the better.

Serves 8

8 mackerel fillets, pin boned

For the dry cure:

100g granulated sugar

75g coarse sea salt

1 teaspoon coarse black pepper

grated zest of 1 lemon

1 Mix all the cure ingredients together. Lay the mackerel fillets, skin-side down, in a dish. Prick with a fork and cover with the curing mixture. Cover the dish and leave in the fridge overnight, or for up to 48 hours if you want them very dry.

2 Remove from the fridge and wash off all the curing mixture under cold running water. Dry well, place in a covered dish and return to the fridge until ready to serve. Serve with potato salad or a leafy salad.

FISH

This chapter features many of the classic
fish dishes I learned to cook years ago. Now that
overfishing has led to dangerously low stocks
in some cases, we need to take care to buy our
fish from sustainable sources. Your fishmonger
should be able to tell you all you need to know
and, if necessary, suggest an alternative — look
for sustainable labels if you're buying in a
supermarket. One of the great things about fish
is that many of them are interchangeable, so
pollack, for example, which is plentiful, can take
the place of cod. Learning how to fillet a fish is
a great skill to acquire; not only is it economical,
but you can also use the bones to make stock.

This is effectively a modern version of that great dish goujons of sole — served slightly bigger and spiced up for the twenty-first century. Any other firm, white flat fish would also work well.

DOVER SOLE IN A SPICY COATING

with tartare sauce

To skin and fillet a flat fish, follow steps 1 to 9
To make mayonnaise, follow steps 10 to 17

SERVES 4

1 large Dover sole or lemon sole

200g fresh fine white breadcrumbs (without crusts)

75g Parmesan cheese, freshly and finely grated

3 tablespoons very finely chopped parsley

1 teaspoon ground cumin

½ teaspoon chilli powder

3 eggs

100g plain flour

sunflower oil for deep-frying

1 lemon, cut lengthways into 6 or 8 wedges

sea salt and black pepper

FOR THE TARTARE SAUCE (MAKES ABOUT 400ML):

2 egg yolks

1 teaspoon Dijon mustard

300ml sunflower oil

¾ teaspoon fine sea salt

2 tablespoons lemon juice, or to taste

2 teaspoons very finely chopped shallot

2 teaspoons finely chopped gherkins

2 teaspoons finely chopped capers

1 tablespoon finely chopped chives

1 tablespoon finely chopped parsley

1 Using scissors, cut off the frill that runs along both sides of the fish.

2 Lay the fish, dark skin-side up, on a board. Then, using a filleting knife, make an incision in the skin across the tail.

3 Lift up just enough skin to grasp with your fingers.

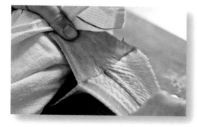

4 Holding the skin in a cloth for a firmer grip, pull it away quickly in one piece, as if ripping off a plaster.

5 The skin is firmly attached, so keep the heel of one hand on the tail while you use all your strength to pull the skin off with the other hand. Turn the fish over and repeat with the white skin side.

6 Cut off the head, remove the blood vessels it leaves behind, and also remove any roes.

7 Using the point of the knife, cut along the backbone of the fish.

8 Working on one side of the backbone, use the flexible side of the knife to slice the flesh away from the bones in long, sweeping strokes.

9 Remove the fillet and repeat on the other side of the backbone, then turn over and repeat on the other side. You should have 4 perfect fillets.

10 For the tartare sauce, first make a mayonnaise. Put a mixing bowl on a folded cloth to prevent it moving while you whisk.

11 Put the egg yolks and mustard in the bowl and whisk until they are combined.

12 Pour the oil into a jug and stand a spoon in it.

13 Lift the spoon out of the jug and hold it over the yolks; this will ensure that you add just the right amount of oil drop by drop.

14 Whisk constantly as you add the drops of oil. When the mixture emulsifies, pour in the oil in a very slow, steady stream.

15 If at any stage the mixture becomes too thick to whisk, add a drop of cold water or lemon juice.

16 When all the oil has been added and you have a smooth, glossy mayonnaise, season with the salt and add lemon juice to taste.

17 If you're not using the mayonnaise straight away, cover and store it in the fridge.

18 To make the tartare sauce, stir the shallot, gherkins, capers, herbs and some black pepper into the mayonnaise.

19 Mix together the breadcrumbs, Parmesan, parsley, cumin, chilli powder and salt and pepper in a bowl, then transfer to a shallow dish.

20 Beat the eggs well in a separate shallow dish. Put the flour into another shallow dish.

21 Cut the fish fillets in half at an angle. Dip each fillet in turn first into the flour, then into the beaten egg and finally into the breadcrumb mixture.

22 Pour enough oil for deep-frying into a deep-fat fryer or large, deep saucepan and heat to 170°C. Carefully add 4 pieces of the fish, making sure they don't touch.

23 Cook until golden brown, then remove with a slotted spoon.

24 Drain the goujons on kitchen paper and keep warm. Repeat with the remaining pieces of fish. Serve with the lemon for squeezing over and the tartare sauce

Dover sole in a spicy coating variations

Dover Sole in a Spicy Dill Coating – follow the recipe on pages 156–158, adding 3 tablespoons of chopped dill to the breadcrumb mixture.

Dover Sole in a Tarragon and Chilli Coating – follow the recipe on pages 156–158, omitting the parsley and cumin from the breadcrumb mixture and instead add 2 tablespoons chopped tarragon.

Dover Sole in a Curry Coating – follow the recipe on pages 156–158, omitting the chilli and cumin from the breadcrumb mixture and instead add 1 teaspoon each of turmeric and ground cumin, 2 teaspoons ground coriander, ¼ teaspoon each ground white pepper, crushed cardamom seeds and cayenne pepper, plus a pinch of nutmeg.

TIPS AND IDEAS

■ Flat fish such as Dover sole have 4 fillets, one on either side of the backbone, both on top and underneath. With a big fish, that means you have 4 lovely natural portions.

■ It's a good idea to fillet fish yourself, as it means you end up with all the bones, from which you can make a simple stock. Even if you ask your fishmonger to do the filleting for you, always ask for the bones.

■ Once the fish is coated, you can keep it in the fridge for several hours until you are ready to cook; you can even freeze it.

■ The fish can be deep-fried in advance, if necessary, then heated through in the oven.

HOW TO COOK A PERFECT PIECE OF FISH

Put a heavy-based frying pan over a medium-high heat and add a little olive oil. Make sure the fish has been properly scaled (see page 173, tips) and run your fingers over the flesh to check for pin bones. Season the fish with salt and white pepper. Dip the skin into a little flour so it is only lightly dusted – the skin tends to be very thin, so the flour forms a protective coating. Place the fish in the hot oil, skin side-down, and leave until it is golden and crisp underneath – this can take about 4 minutes, depending on the thickness of the flesh. Do not move it around the pan or you will break the crust that is forming. The fillet will begin to change colour up the sides as it cooks. Turn it over and leave to cook for a couple more minutes, then remove the pan from the heat and let the fish rest for 3 minutes before serving.

If cooking a whole fish, such as a trout, use a knife to scape it clean, then flour it lightly as above. Score it 3 times on either side with a sharp knife, then fry in hot oil for 4–5 minutes per side.

How to tell when fish is done:

■ In fillets or steaks, the flesh will have turned opaque and milky. It should come off in large flakes when teased with a knife.

■ Whole fish are done when the skin peels off easily. You can also insert a knife near the backbone to check that the flesh flakes.

LEMON SOLE WITH BASIL AND PRAWN STUFFING

This is a classic way of preparing lemon sole, using it rather like a waistcoat by removing the bone from the centre and stuffing it. It's definitely a dinner-party dish but you can prepare it in the morning or even the night before. This dish is also good with brill.

Serves 4

2 medium lemon soles, weighing about 600–700g each

40g unsalted butter, melted, plus extra for greasing

sea salt and black pepper

For the stuffing:

300g raw peeled tiger prawns, finely chopped

200g raw salmon, finely chopped

100g crème fraîche or ricotta cheese

16 basil leaves, chopped

3 tablespoons chopped flat-leaf parsley

1 tablespoon finely chopped chives

For the ginger and lemongrass butter sauce:

250ml white wine

1 lemongrass stalk, bashed and chopped

1.5cm piece of fresh ginger, finely chopped

250g cold unsalted butter, diced

10 basil leaves

1 Lemon soles are slightly smaller than Dover soles, but trim them as described on page 157, steps 1 and 6. I like to keep the skin on because I think it gives a better result if you remove it after the fish is cooked, but you could remove it at this stage to make it quicker to serve (see page 157, steps 2–5).

2 On the dark skin side, ease the fillets off the bones on either side of the backbone as described on page 157, steps 7 and 8, but keep them attached along the outer edge of the fish. Use your filleting knife to work under the backbone to release the other 2 fillets from underneath. Cut the backbone at the tail end and remove it completely. Prepare the other sole in the same way. You will end up with 4 'pockets' in which to put the stuffing.

3 To make the stuffing, put the prawns and salmon into a bowl. Fold in the crème fraîche or ricotta and all the herbs. Season with salt and pepper. Whiz with a hand blender for 5 seconds, until well combined but retaining some texture.

4 Place the lemon sole on a buttered baking tray. Fold back the top fillets to expose the bottom fillets, season with salt and pepper and then spoon in the stuffing. Replace the top fillets to cover the stuffing, leaving a small gap in the middle. Brush the fish with melted butter, then cover with foil, place in an oven preheated to 190°C/Gas Mark 5 and cook for 20 minutes.

5 Meanwhile, make the sauce. Put the wine, lemongrass and ginger into a saucepan and simmer until reduced to 4 tablespoons. Strain through a fine sieve into a small saucepan. Take off the heat, add the butter a few pieces at a time, whisking continuously. Return to the heat and bring to a simmer. Season well and add the basil leaves.

6 Check whether the fish is firm to the touch. If not, cook for a further 5 minutes. When ready, remove from the oven and leave to rest for 5 minutes. Carefully remove the skin, any side bones and the tail. Place the fish onto a serving platter and let people help themselves. Serve with the sauce and some new potatoes.

DOVER SOLE MEUNIÈRE

I couldn't possibly leave out this dish. It is one of the all-time greats. I have strayed from the traditional version only by omitting the flour for coating the fish – I simply don't think it needs it. Serve with new potatoes, preferably Jersey Royals.

Serves 2

2 Dover soles, weighing about 500g each

1 tablespoon sunflower oil

90g unsalted butter

1 rounded tablespoon finely chopped curly parsley

juice of 1 lemon

sea salt and black pepper

1 Trim the soles and remove the skin as described on page 157, steps 1–6.

2 Heat the oil in a frying pan, add 60g of the butter and let it melt. Add the fish and cook over a medium-low heat for 4 minutes. Turn it over gently and cook for a further 4 minutes.

3 Carefully remove the fish from the frying pan and place on a flat surface. With the point of your filleting knife, cut along the backbone, then lift the fillet carefully to one side. Repeat with the other side, and now lift out the backbone. It should come out in one piece. Slide the 2 fillets back into place.

4 Wipe out the frying pan with kitchen paper. Add the parsley and lemon juice to the pan with the remaining butter and cook just until it starts to smell slightly nutty. Remove it quickly from the heat and pour it over the fish. Serve immediately.

GRILLED PLAICE WITH SAUCE VIERGE

Grilling flat fish such as plaice is very easy to do, and the best way to serve it is with a simple herb sauce. If you can't buy plaice, try using haddock or cod instead.

Serves 4

4 large plaice fillets

60g unsalted butter, melted, plus extra for greasing

sea salt and black pepper

For the sauce vierge:

200ml olive oil

juice of 1 lemon

2 tomatoes, skinned (see page 278, step 1), deseeded and chopped

2 tablespoons chopped flat-leaf parsley

2 tablespoons chopped coriander

12 basil leaves, torn into pieces

1 Place the fillets, skin-side down, on a buttered baking tray, brush with melted butter and season with salt and pepper.

2 To make the sauce, put the oil and lemon juice into a pan with the tomatoes, parsley, coriander and basil and heat gently.

3 Cook the fillets under a preheated medium grill for 2–3 minutes. Serve with the sauce vierge on top.

GRILLED BRILL WITH PARSLEY BUTTER AND CAPER SAUCE

If you can get one large brill weighing about a kilo, you can serve it whole at the table and it looks beautiful. You will need to bake it in the oven at 180°C/Gas Mark 4 for 20–25 minutes. You could substitute plaice for the brill if you like.

Serves 4

2 brill, weighing about 600g each

60g unsalted butter, melted, plus extra for greasing

For the parsley butter and caper sauce:

1 lemon, segmented (see page 41, step 27)

200ml chicken or fish stock

2 tablespoons capers, drained

2 tablespoons finely diced shallots

1 tablespoon finely chopped flat-leaf parsley

150g unsalted butter, cut into cubes

sea salt and black pepper

1 Prepare and trim the brill as described on page 157, steps 1–6. Make sure the dark skin is scaled (see page 173, tips). Cut 3 slits through the skin, but only just into the flesh, on either side of the backbone, like the ribs of a leaf. Place the fish on a buttered baking tray and brush the top with plenty of melted butter. Cook under a preheated medium grill and cook for 10–12 minutes, until firm to the touch.

2 Meanwhile, make the sauce. Cut the lemon segments into small pieces. Put the stock, capers, lemon pieces, shallots and parsley into a saucepan and bring to the boil. Season well with salt and pepper, then whisk in the butter a little at a time. Serve the sauce as soon as it is ready.

3 Serve the fish with Ribbon Courgettes (page 33) and the sauce over the top.

HALIBUT IN A BAG WITH FENNEL, TOMATOES, BLACK GRAPES AND BASIL

Grapes with fish is an underused combination. This is a clean and simple dish to make because the fish is just wrapped in foil with its flavourings and baked in the oven. I like to start it off in a frying pan, so the tomatoes begin to cook before it goes in the oven. Any white fish could be cooked in the same way.

Serves 4

1 small fennel bulb, very thinly sliced

4 tablespoons extra virgin olive oil

4 ripe plum tomatoes, sliced

4 halibut fillets, weighing about 170g each

16 seedless black grapes, halved

4 sprigs of thyme

12 basil leaves

250g wild rocket

1 frisée lettuce

1 quantity of Vinaigrette (see page 136)

sea salt and black pepper

1 Bring a saucepan of water to the boil, add the fennel and cook for 5 minutes. Drain well, refresh in cold water and pat dry.

2 Cut four 25cm square sheets of thick foil. Put 1 tablespoon olive oil in the centre of each sheet. Make a bed of sliced tomato on each one, then divide the fennel among them and season with salt and pepper. Place the halibut on top and season again, then sprinkle over the black grapes, thyme and basil. Fold over the foil and crimp the edges, making sure you seal them well.

3 Put the foil bags in a dry, ovenproof frying pan over a medium heat and cook for 2 minutes. Place in an oven preheated to 180°C/Gas Mark 4 and cook for a further 8 minutes.

4 Prepare a salad with the rocket and frisée and toss in the vinaigrette. Serve the fish in large pasta bowls, as there are lots of juices, with the salad alongside.

ROAST HADDOCK WITH BEURRE BLANC

You could adapt this recipe for cod, sea bass or monkfish — in fact, any firm white fish would do. It looks so pretty on the plate with its lovely summery accompaniment of Little Gem lettuce and peas.

Serves 4

sunflower oil

4 thick pieces of haddock fillet, weighing about 180g each

2 teaspoons crushed black pepper

For the vegetables:

12 shallots

50g unsalted butter

4 rashers of bacon, cut into small pieces

1 tablespoon sugar

2 tablespoons chicken stock

2 Little Gem lettuces, shredded

300g petit pois

sea salt and black pepper

chopped chives, to garnish

For the beurre blanc sauce:

100ml white wine

1 tablespoon finely chopped shallot

1 tablespoon double cream

250g unsalted butter, cut into cubes

juice of ½ lemon

white pepper

1 First prepare the vegetables. Bring a saucepan of water to the boil, add the shallots and cook for 7 minutes, until tender. Remove and drain well.

2 Melt 30g of the butter in a frying pan, add the bacon and fry until crispy. Remove the bacon and set aside, then add the shallots to the pan and cook over a low heat until golden, shaking the pan occasionally. Add the sugar and stock, then toss in the shredded lettuce, the peas and bacon. Season with salt and pepper and add the remaining butter. Keep warm.

3 To make the beurre blanc sauce, put the wine and shallot in a saucepan, bring to the boil and reduce to 1 tablespoon. Add the cream and remove from the heat. Whisk in the butter bit by bit to emulsify it, then season with the lemon juice, salt and white pepper. Keep warm.

4 Heat a little oil in a non-stick ovenproof frying pan until just hot. Season the haddock all over with salt and the crushed pepper, place in the pan and cook, skin-side down, for 2 minutes, until brown. Turn it over, then place the pan in an oven preheated to 180°C/Gas Mark 4 and continue cooking for about 7 minutes. When done, the fish should have an opaque, milky and succulent appearance.

5 Place some vegetables on each serving plate in an attractive way, sprinkle with the chives, then put the fish in the centre and pour the sauce around it.

POACHED TURBOT WITH SPINACH AND CREAMED CHIVE POTATOES

Creamed potatoes are usually thought of as something to serve with meat but they go extremely well with fish. Braising the fish keeps it wonderfully moist. This dish would also work well using halibut or brill instead of the turbot.

Serves 4

60g unsalted butter, plus extra for greasing

1 small shallot, finely diced

100g button mushrooms, sliced

juice of ½ lemon

250ml fish stock

4 turbot fillets, weighing about 150g each

100ml double cream

Beurre Manié (see page 70, tips), made with 15g soft unsalted butter and 15g plain flour (optional)

a pinch of sugar

3 tablespoons finely chopped chives

1 quantity of Creamed Potatoes (see page 86)

sea salt and white pepper

For the spinach:

30g unsalted butter

250g fresh spinach

juice of ¼ lemon

a pinch of nutmeg

1 Melt 30g of the butter in a small saucepan, add the shallot and cook until softened, without browning. Add the mushrooms, lemon juice and stock and simmer for 30 seconds. Transfer the mixture to a baking dish and put the turbot fillets on top, skin-side up. Melt the remaining butter and brush over the fish. Season well with salt and white pepper, then cover with a piece of buttered greaseproof paper. Place in an oven preheated to 180°C/Gas Mark 4 and cook for 6–8 minutes.

2 Transfer the turbot to a dish and keep warm. Pour the mushroom mixture into a saucepan, add the cream and simmer to reduce to a sauce-like consistency. If necessary, thicken with the *beurre manié*, whisking it into the sauce a small piece at a time to thicken it – you might not need it all. Season with salt and white pepper and a pinch of sugar.

3 To prepare the spinach, melt the butter in a frying pan, add all the ingredients plus salt and pepper and cook until the spinach has wilted. Meanwhile, stir the chives into the Creamed Potatoes.

4 To serve, place a large metal ring or pastry cutter in the middle of each plate, fill with creamed potatoes, then remove the ring. Top with some spinach and the turbot and pour some of the sauce around it.

Filleting a round fish, such as salmon, requires a slightly different method than for flat fish. This is a spectacular party piece that can be prepared the day before.

SALMON EN CROÛTE

To fillet the salmon, follow steps 1 to 3
To skin the salmon, follow steps 5 to 8

SERVES 12

1 salmon, weighing about 2.5kg, cleaned

unsalted butter, for greasing

1 lemon, sliced

3 bay leaves

2 sprigs of curly parsley

5 black peppercorns

800g puff pastry

plain flour for dusting

2 eggs, beaten, to seal and glaze

sea salt and black pepper

FOR THE PANCAKES:

60g plain flour

1 egg, beaten

175ml full-fat milk

25g unsalted butter, melted

olive oil for frying, if needed

FOR THE SALMON MOUSSE:

1 tablespoon olive oil

1 onion, finely chopped

150g button mushrooms, chopped

400g salmon fillet (see step 9 opposite)

1 egg white

300ml double cream

2 tablespoons finely chopped curly parsley

75g cooked basmati rice

1 Using a filleting knife, which has a pointed, flexible blade, cut around the head and across the tail, cutting through the flesh to the bone.

2 Starting from the head end, cut along the back of the fish in a single, clean stroke, just above the backbone.

3 Using the point of the knife, gradually release the flesh from the bones in long, sweeping strokes until the fillet is completely removed. Turn the fish over and repeat on the other side.

4 Clean the fillets of any white fatty parts and remove the pin bones with tweezers.

5 To remove the skin, lay one fillet, skin-side down, on the work surface, holding the tail end very firmly in one hand.

6 Use the knife in your other hand to lift a small area of the flesh away from the skin.

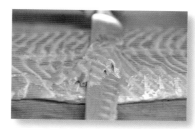

7 Holding the knife almost flat, cut between the flesh and skin, using a sawing action to remove the filllet in one piece.

8 Remove any brown fat on the underside of the fillet, slicing it off as thinly as possible. Repeat steps 3–8 with the other fillet.

9 Set aside a 700g piece of salmon for the croûte and an additional 400g for the mousse. Cut the rest into portions and freeze.

10 To cook the salmon, take a large, doubled sheet of foil and grease all over with butter.

11 Place the larger piece of salmon on the foil, then top with the lemon slices, bay leaves, parsley and peppercorns.

12 Bring up the sides of the foil and crimp to seal, then place on a baking tray. Place in an oven preheated to 200°C/Gas Mark 6 and bake for about 20 minutes.

TIPS AND IDEAS

■ If you are cooking salmon or other round fish with the skin on, you will need to scale it. Holding the fish by the tail, scrape towards the head with the back of a knife so you are working against the way the scales lie. This job can also be done with metal fish scalers.

■ Cooking the salmon before wrapping it in the pastry might seem like a complication too many, but I like to do so because otherwise the fish can create too much moisture within the pastry case. The pancakes also help to keep the pastry dry.

■ The dish can be assembled in advance right up to step 33, where it is wrapped in pastry (but not glazed), then frozen. Thaw in the fridge, then brush with egg and cook as in steps 35 and 36.

■ If you prefer, you could make the mixture into individual parcels. In this case, you won't need the pancakes.

■ Before making the mousse, chill the ingredients well to help prevent the mixture separating when you process it.

■ Double-check that the pastry is well sealed all around the edges so that the filling won't leak out during cooking.

■ If you want to do a quick version of this dish, you can buy salmon fillets and even ready-made pancakes.

salmon en croûte variations

Salmon and White Fish en Croûte – follow the recipe on pages 168–171, replacing half the salmon for the mousse with 200g white fish, such as whiting or lemon sole.

Salmon en Croûte with Spinach – cook 250g fresh spinach in a knob of unsalted butter with some salt and pepper for 2–3 minutes, until wilted. Drain well and make sure it is dry by patting it with a cloth. Follow the recipe on pages 168–171, adding the spinach to one-quarter of the salmon mousse and layering it in the centre of the salmon.

Salmon Coulibiac – hard-boil 5 eggs, peel them and cut in half lengthways. Follow the recipe on pages 168–171, putting the eggs, flat-side down, in a long line between the 2 layers of salmon, with the mousse around the eggs.

Salmon en Croûte with Wild Mushrooms – finely chop 250g wild mushrooms and cook them in 60g unsalted butter in a large frying pan until tender, seasoning with salt and pepper. Drain well and then leave them to cool on a cloth to soak up any excess liquid. Follow the recipe on pages 168–171, adding the mushrooms to one-quarter of the mousse mixture and layering it in the centre of the salmon.

SEARED RED MULLET WITH TABBOULEH AND CRISPY GARLIC

Serves 4

8 red mullet fillets, weighing about 180g each

plain flour, seasoned with salt and black pepper, for dusting

olive oil

watercress, to garnish

For the tabbouleh:

200g bulgur wheat

450g tomatoes, skinned (see page 278, step 1), deseeded and finely diced

1 onion, finely diced

juice of 2 lemons

6 tablespoons shredded mint leaves

2 tablespoons extra virgin olive oil

sea salt and black pepper

For the crispy garlic:

8 garlic cloves

sunflower oil for deep-frying

1 First make the tabbouleh. Rinse the bulgur wheat in cold water, then place in a bowl, cover with boiling water and cling film and leave for 20 minutes. Fluff up with a fork, add the other ingredients and season well with salt and pepper.

2 To make the crispy garlic, heat 2cm oil in a deep-fat fryer or deep saucepan to 140°C. Slice the garlic thinly and fry in batches for about 8 minutes or until pale golden. Drain on kitchen paper.

3 Dust the mullet in the seasoned flour, shaking off any excess. Heat a little oil in a frying pan over a medium heat, add the mullet, skin-side down, and cook for 1 minute, until golden brown. Turn over and cook for a further minute. Remove and allow to rest for 3 minutes.

4 To serve, place a circle of tabbouleh on each serving plate, place the mullet on top, sprinkle with crispy garlic and garnish with watercress.

ROAST COD WITH CANNELLINI BEANS AND PANCETTA

Serves 4

4 thick cod fillets, weighing about 160g each

olive oil

For the crispy sage:

8 sage leaves

sunflower oil for deep-frying

For the beans:

olive oil

1 onion, finely chopped

100g pancetta, chopped

1 garlic clove, finely chopped

200g cooked cannellini beans

250ml chicken stock

2 tomatoes, skinned (see page 278, step 1), deseeded and diced

2 tablespoons chopped mixed flat-leaf parsley, marjoram and oregano

sea salt and black pepper

1 To prepare the beans, heat a little olive oil in a large saucepan, add the onion and cook until softened. Add the pancetta and garlic and cook for 2 more minutes. Now add the beans, pour in the stock and simmer for 15 minutes. Finally, add the tomatoes and cook for a further 5 minutes. Just before serving, season well with salt and pepper and add the herbs.

2 To prepare the crispy sage, heat 2cm oil in a deep-fat fryer or deep saucepan to 170°C. Add the sage and fry for 30 seconds, until crisp and golden. Drain on kitchen paper.

3 To cook the fish, heat a little olive oil in a non-stick frying pan and add the cod, skin-side down. Cook for 2 minutes, then transfer to a baking dish, skin-side up. Place in an oven preheated to 220°C/Gas Mark 7 and cook for about 8 minutes. Serve the cod, skin-side up, on the beans, and top with the crispy sage.

BAKED COD WITH ROAST ROOT VEGETABLES AND THYME AND ROSEMARY SAUCE

I used to cook fish with root vegetables a lot when I worked in the south of France. I've been partial to the combination ever since. Any white fish could be baked in the same way.

Serves 4

4 cod fillets, weighing about 180g each

olive oil

sea salt and black pepper

For the root vegetables:

8 unpeeled slices of pumpkin, about 8cm long and 2cm thick

1 large parsnip, quartered

2 large carrots, halved lengthways

extra virgin olive oil

2 tablespoons chopped mixed thyme and rosemary

For the sauce:

4 tablespoons white wine

1 tablespoon white wine vinegar

1 shallot, finely chopped

2 tomatoes, roughly chopped

200ml fish stock

4 sprigs of thyme

2 sprigs of rosemary

1 bay leaf

100g cold unsalted butter, cut into cubes

1 Put the root vegetables on a baking tray with plenty of olive oil, the herbs and salt. Place in an oven preheated to 180°C/Gas Mark 4 and cook for 40–50 minutes, until golden.

2 To make the sauce, put the wine and vinegar into a small saucepan, add the shallot and bring to the boil. Reduce to 2 tablespoons, then add the chopped tomatoes, fish stock and herbs and simmer to reduce to 100ml. Whisk in the butter a bit at a time to thicken the sauce. Keep simmering until it is quite thick. Strain before serving.

3 To cook the cod, heat a little oil in a frying pan with until medium-hot. Add the cod, skin-side down, and cook for 2 minutes. Transfer to a baking tray, skin-side up, and place in the oven for about 8 minutes. Serve with the roast root vegetables and the sauce poured around it.

CAJUN-SCENTED MONKFISH WITH SUMMER VEGETABLES

This is a lovely way to enjoy summer vegetables, and the mint makes it really refreshing. The monkfish wrapped in Parma ham can be eaten all year round – try it with the Tabbouleh on page 176 or with the Saffron Risotto on page 88, omitting the bone marrow. You could adapt this recipe for pollack or cod.

Serves 4

4 monkfish fillets, weighing about 150g each

4 slices of Parma ham

olive oil

For the Cajun spices:

½ teaspoon coarse sea salt

½ teaspoon smoked paprika

¼ teaspoon chilli powder

½ teaspoon ground black pepper

½ teaspoon garlic salt

For the summer vegetables:

1kg broad beans in their pods, shelled (300g shelled weight)

500g fresh peas in their pods, shelled (150g shelled weight)

250g baby carrots

40g unsalted butter

2 tablespoons olive oil

8 spring onions, sliced

1 tablespoon chopped curly parsley

2 tablespoons chopped mint

a pinch of sugar

sea salt and black pepper

1 Remove any membranes from the monkfish. To do this, cut between the membrane and the fish with the knife angled flat, using a sawing motion as if skinning the fillet. The idea is to end up with a clean piece of fish. Combine all the Cajun spices in a bowl, then rub the mixture into the monkfish, turning it a few times to coat well. Wrap each fillet in a slice of Parma ham, place on a tray and set aside in the fridge.

2 Meanwhile, prepare the vegetables. Bring a pan of water to the boil, add the broad beans and cook for 1 minute. Drain and refresh in cold water, then drain again. Peel off the skins and put the beans in a bowl. Cook the peas in boiling water for 2 minutes. Drain and refresh in cold water, then drain again. Cook the carrots in boiling water for 3 minutes or until tender, then drain.

3 Melt the butter in a large frying pan, add the oil and spring onions and cook for 30 seconds, until softened, then add the carrots, peas and beans. Stir in the herbs and sugar and season with salt and pepper.

4 Heat a little oil in a non-stick frying pan, add the wrapped monkfish, seam-side down, and cook, turning, until browned on all sides. Transfer to a baking tray and place in an oven preheated to 180°C/ Gas Mark 4 for 7 minutes. Remove and allow to rest for 5 minutes. Serve sliced into 3 pieces on the summer vegetables.

CARPACCIO OF SEA BASS WITH A PICKLED CARROT SALAD

I got the idea for this from a Japanese lady who came to one of my cookery classes. She would flatten out raw langoustines and serve them dressed with a little olive oil, lemon juice and salt. I had some sea bass and suggested to her that we try the same technique with it. The fish has to be extremely fresh and you will need a very sharp, flexible knife. Put the fish in the freezer briefly to firm it up a little so it will be easier to slice. Raw tuna could be prepared in the same way.

Serves 4

4 large carrots, peeled

1 tablespoon white wine vinegar

1 piece of stem ginger, finely chopped

1 tablespoon caster sugar

4 sea bass fillets, weighing about 150g each

8 radishes, thinly sliced

3 spring onions, cut into fine strips

4 sprigs of dill, chopped

grated zest of 2 limes

olive oil for sprinkling

sea salt

For the sauce:

30ml sake

50ml mirin

100ml soy sauce

1 teaspoon sugar

1 Grate the carrots very finely. Put them in a colander, sprinkle with some salt and leave to drain for 30 minutes, turning occasionally to release the liquid. Rinse off the salt and pat dry with kitchen paper. Put the carrots into a bowl with the vinegar, stem ginger and sugar and set aside while you start on the fish.

2 Make sure there are no bones left in the fish (see page 143, step 2). Hold each fillet by the tail, skin-side down, and slice it very thinly. Arrange the slices fanned out in a circle on each plate, leaving a round gap in the middle. If you have a 5cm metal ring or pastry cutter, use it as a template to achieve a neat presentation. Cover with cling film and place in the fridge until required.

3 Half an hour before you want to eat, drain the carrot in a colander and make a circular arrangement with the radish slices in the centre of each plate (inside the ring if you are using one), see picture opposite.

4 Mix together all the ingredients for the sauce in a small bowl and set aside.

5 Scatter the fish with spring onions and dill, then finally sprinkle with the lime zest and a little olive oil. Offer the sauce seperately as a dip.

SEARED SEA BASS WITH POTATO AND SPINACH CAKES AND TOMATO SALSA

A delicious and substantial dish. The sea bass also goes well with a rice salad instead of the potato cakes. This recipe is also wonderful using grey mullet instead of sea bass.

Serves 4

4 sea bass fillets, weighing about 120g each

plain flour for dusting

30g unsalted butter

1 tablespoon olive oil

For the tomato salsa:

1 red pepper, skinned (see page 32, step 1), deseeded and very finely chopped

4 large vine tomatoes, skinned (see page 278, step 1), deseeded and finely diced

1 banana shallot, very finely diced

1 teaspoon very finely chopped red chilli

1 garlic clove, finely chopped

1 lime, segmented (see page 41, step 27) and finely chopped

4 tablespoons olive oil

a pinch of sugar

sea salt and white pepper

For the potato and spinach cakes:

500g potatoes, peeled and cut into equal pieces

20g unsalted butter

150g fresh spinach

20g dill, chopped (optional)

30g Parmesan cheese, freshly grated

100g Wensleydale cheese, finely grated

1 egg yolk

150g plain flour

3 eggs, lightly beaten

200g white breadcrumbs

sunflower oil for shallow frying

1 First make the salsa. Put all the ingredients into a small saucepan; place over a medium heat for 1 minute to bring out the flavours. Set aside to cool.

2 To make the spinach cakes, bring a saucepan of salted water to the boil, add the potatoes and cook until soft. Drain well. Melt the butter in a frying pan with 2 tablespoons water, add the spinach and cook until wilted. Drain thoroughly, pressing to make sure the spinach is very dry. Put the potatoes, spinach, dill, if using, cheeses and egg yolk in a bowl, mix well and season with salt and pepper. Shape into 4 cakes about 8cm wide and 2cm thick, then place on a tray and set in the fridge for at least 2 hours.

3 Put the flour, beaten eggs and breadcrumbs into 3 separate bowls. Coat the cakes with the flour, then the egg, then the breadcrumbs. Repeat this step if you'd like the cakes to have a thicker coating.

4 Heat 1.5cm of sunflower oil in a frying pan over a medium heat. Add the cakes and cook for about 1 minute on each side, until golden brown. Transfer to a baking tray and place in an oven preheated to 190°C/Gas Mark 5. Bake for 6–8 minutes while you cook the fish.

5 Cut 5 slits in the skin of the sea bass. Dust the skin side only in the flour, then shake off as much as possible.

6 Melt the butter with the oil in a frying pan over a medium heat and add the sea bass, skin-side down. Press with a spatula so the fish lies flat and cook for 1–2 minutes, until golden brown. Turn it over and cook for another minute, then remove and allow to rest for 2 minutes. If you want to prepare the fish in advance, cook the skin side until crisp, then cook the other side for just 10 seconds. When you're ready to serve, place the part-cooked fish in an oven preheated to 220°C/Gas Mark 7 for 2 minutes. Serve with the cakes and the tomato salsa.

SEA BASS IN A SALT CRUST WITH BRAISED FENNEL

Cooking fish in a salt crust keeps it perfectly moist — and, surprisingly, it doesn't taste of salt. It looks very attractive when it comes out of the oven but serving it is a messy job. Don't worry; it will taste wonderful. Get the largest sea bass you can find. Grey mullet can also be cooked in this way.

Serves 2

1 sea bass, weighing about 700g, cleaned and scaled (see page 173, tips)

1kg fine cooking salt

2 small egg whites

1 lemon

1 tablespoon finely chopped rosemary and thyme

½ quantity of Creamed Potatoes (see page 86)

sea salt and black pepper

chervil or dill, to garnish

For the braised fennel:

1 large fennel bulb or 2 small ones

40g unsalted butter, plus extra for greasing

4 tablespoons freshly grated Parmesan cheese

white pepper

1 Wash the sea bass to remove any blood and dry well. Mix the fine salt and egg whites in a bowl: if they do not form a paste, add a little water and stir until they do.

2 Cut 3 thin slices off the lemon, reserving the rest for the garnish. Place the slices in the cavity of the fish with the chopped herbs and season with salt and pepper. If the fennel has any leafy fronds, chop these up and place inside the sea bass too.

3 Spread one-third of the salt paste on to a baking tray, put the fish on top and cover with the rest of the paste, making sure you don't leave any gaps.

4 Place in an oven preheated to 200°C/Gas Mark 6 and cook for about 30 minutes. Remove from the oven and, using a knife, carefully crack the salt crust open and peel off the skin. Carefully transfer the fish to a serving dish. Leave the oven on.

5 While the fish is cooking, cut the fennel into 8 pieces if large, or 6 pieces if small, keeping the root on. Bring a large pan of water to the boil, add the fennel and simmer for 7 minutes, until soft, then drain well. Butter a small ovenproof dish, add the cooked fennel, then cover in the butter and season with salt and white pepper. Sprinkle the Parmesan on top and bake in the oven for 25 minutes, until golden brown.

6 Serve the sea bass with the baked fennel and Creamed Potatoes (see page 86), garnished with lemon wedges and chervil or dill.

STEAMED WHOLE SEA BASS WITH GINGER AND SPRING ONIONS

This is such a healthy dish and it also works well with grey mullet. If the fish doesn't fit in your steamer, you can curl it around but remember, it will stay curled after cooking. You could also cook it in a fish kettle.

Serves 4

1 sea bass, weighing about 800g, cleaned and scaled (see page 173, tips)

2 tablespoons soy sauce

2 teaspoons sesame oil

1 tablespoon sherry

1 teaspoon sugar

sunflower oil

2cm piece of fresh ginger, cut into fine strips

6 spring onions, cut into fine strips

1 Score the top of the fish, just cutting into the flesh, not all the way through it. Place the fish in a large dish.

2 In a bowl, mix together the soy sauce, sesame oil, sherry and sugar. Pour over the fish, then cover and leave to marinate in the fridge for at least 2 hours, turning occasionally.

3 Place a heatproof plate in a large steamer, then place the sea bass on top and pour over the marinade. Cook for 10 minutes, until just cooked through. Remove from the heat.

4 Heat a little sunflower oil in a frying pan over a high heat, and when the oil is hot add the ginger. Cook for 1 minute, until softened. Add the spring onions, the marinade and all the fish juices and simmer for 2 minutes. Transfer the fish to a serving platter, pour over the sauce and serve.

MACKEREL ESCABECHE

Cook the day before if possible, as the fish really improves after marinating overnight.

Serves 4

2 teaspoons coriander seeds, crushed

2 teaspoons cumin seeds, crushed

1 shallot, very thinly sliced

1 carrot, very thinly sliced

½ fennel bulb, thinly sliced

3 garlic cloves, crushed

200ml extra virgin olive oil

2 tablespoons white wine vinegar

juice of 1 large orange

a large pinch of saffron strands

1 teaspoon sugar

4 large mackerel fillets, pin bones removed (see page 143, step 2)

3 tablespoons plain flour

olive oil

sea salt and black pepper

flat-leaf parsley, to garnish

1 Put the seeds in a dry frying pan and heat for a minute or two: be careful not to burn them. Add the shallot, carrot, fennel, garlic and 50ml of the extra virgin olive oil. Cook over a low heat for 3 minutes, until softened. Add the remaining oil, the vinegar, orange juice, saffron and sugar, cover and cook gently for 8 minutes. Season with salt and pepper and leave to cool.

2 Cut the mackerel fillets diagonally in two. Season the flour with salt and pepper and dust over the skin side of the fish. Heat a little olive oil in a non-stick frying pan, add the fish, skin-side down, and cook for 1 minute, until crisp and golden. Turn over and cook for just 30 seconds.

3 Spoon the vegetable mixture into a serving dish and place the fish on top. Cover with cling film and place in the fridge for 4 hours before serving, garnished with parsley.

SHELLFISH

Shellfish are one of the wonders of the world, providing some of the sweetest flavours you can get. There's nothing like a fresh crab cooked straight from the sea, or a beautiful, barely cooked scallop served in its shell. It goes without saying that shellfish must be extremely fresh — in some cases, to the point that they have to be sold still alive. All shellfish is best eaten on the day of purchase, and certainly should not be stored in the fridge for more than 24 hours.

I am very wary of buying crab ready dressed as you have no way of knowing how fresh it was when it was cooked — far better to cook and dress your own. If you are cooking the crab yourself, it must be live, in which case it will be sold with rubber bands around its claws — don't remove these, otherwise it might nip you.

CLASSIC DRESSED CRAB

To cook the crab, follow steps 4 to 5
To remove the crabmeat, follow steps 6 to 15

SERVES 1

1 live crab, weighing about 1 kg

juice of ½ lemon

2 teaspoons mayonnaise

2 tablespoons fresh white breadcrumbs

a pinch of cayenne pepper

1 egg, hard-boiled and shelled

1 tablespoon finely chopped curly parsley

sea salt and black pepper

1 Turn your crab upside down to check whether it's female or male: the female has a red oval flap to carry her eggs, and the male has a long vertical tail.

2 Using a thick metal skewer, pierce between the crab's eyes at a 45-degree angle, pushing the skewer right through the head so that it comes out at the base of the two flaps.

3 Bring a very large saucepan of water to the boil with plenty of salt added. Meanwhile, weigh the crab.

4 Add the crab to the pan and cook for 20 minutes if 500g, 25 minutes if 800g, 30 minutes if 1.2kg and 35 minutes if 1.5kg. Drain and leave to cool.

5 To remove the crabmeat, first twist off the 2 large claws, then all the remaining legs.

6 Put the crab sideways on to its head and lightly bang with your fist. The body should just come away from the main shell.

7 Put your thumb underneath the head and then remove it with the 2 side bones (they look rather like a wishbone).

8 Remove and discard the grey lungs, known as dead men's fingers.

9 Using a spoon, scoop out the brown meat and put it into a bowl. Reserve the main outer shell.

10 Hold a large claw at one end and give a firm tap to the shell with the back of a large, heavy knife. The shell will crack and you can pull it apart.

11 Remove the white meat from all parts of the claw and put it into a separate bowl. Repeat with the other claw.

12 Bash the legs with the back of your knife to crack the shells and remove as much meat as possible. Reserve the shells for making Crab Bisque (see page 193).

13 Cut the body in half and remove all the white meat from the crevices where the legs were removed.

14 Check through the white meat to remove any remaining bits of shell – you will need to do this at least twice.

15 You will now have a bowl of brown meat, a bowl of white meat and the main outer shell, plus the other shells for making soup or stock.

16 Season the white meat lightly with 1 teaspoon of the lemon juice, some salt and the mayonnaise.

17 Add the breadcrumbs to the brown meat with the remaining lemon juice and the cayenne, mix well and season with salt and pepper.

18 Separate the hard-boiled egg yolk and egg white. Rub the yolk through a coarse sieve.

19 Then rub the egg white through a clean coarse sieve.

20 On the outer shell you will see what look like dotted lines down the sides. Push down on them with your thumbs and the sides should snap off.

21 Rinse the prepared shell and pat dry.

22 Divide the brown crabmeat in half and spoon it into the sides of the shell. Put the white meat in the centre to fill the shell.

23 Add a row of egg yolk in between the white and brown meat on one side. Then add a row of egg white to separate the meats on the other side.

24 Arrange a row of chopped parsley at an angle across the white meat. Serve at once.

TIPS AND IDEAS

■ Try to buy crabs that are heavy for their size – they will have plenty of meat.

■ Killing the crab is not as daunting as it sounds. An ordinary metal kebab skewer is fine for the job. As long as you drive the skewer through the crab's body, it should be dead within seconds. The shell underneath the crab, near the head, is surprisingly soft.

■ A special crab pick to remove the meat from the legs is useful but not essential – a skewer works almost as well.

■ It's important to pick through the crabmeat really thoroughly with your fingers to get rid of any tiny pieces of shell.

■ Crabmeat freezes very well, and you can also freeze the shells to use in a bisque (see opposite). You can even freeze the whole cooked crab. Don't keep it in the fridge for more than 2 days, though – like all seafood, crab is best eaten very fresh.

CHILLED CHARENTAIS MELON SOUP WITH CRAB SALAD

Melon makes an extremely refreshing soup. The Charentais or Cantaloupe varieties give it a wonderful colour, while the crab adds a touch of luxury. It's perfect for a hot summer's day.

Serves 4

1 Charentais or Cantaloupe melon

¼ medium watermelon

juice of ½ lime, plus a little extra for the crab salad

2 teaspoons sherry vinegar

sea salt and black pepper

For the crab salad:

150g fresh white crabmeat

½ shallot, finely chopped

¼ small cucumber, peeled and finely diced

a few mint leaves, chopped, plus extra to garnish

2 tablespoons mayonnaise

1 Cut the melon and watermelon into quarters and remove the seeds. Cut the flesh into chunks and put into a blender along with the lime juice and the sherry vinegar. Add a small pinch of salt and a good twist of black pepper and blend to a very smooth purée. Pour into a bowl and place in the freezer to chill while you prepare the salad.

2 Put the crabmeat into a bowl and pick out any bits of shell. Add the shallot, cucumber and mint, then stir in the mayonnaise to bind the mixture together. Add a little lime juice and season with salt and pepper.

3 To serve, place a large spoonful of crab salad in the centre of 4 chilled soup bowls. Pour the cold melon soup around the crab and garnish with the reserved mint leaves.

CRAB BISQUE

After you have cooked and prepared your own crabs, use the shells to make this soup. If you don't want to make it straight away, the shells will keep in the freezer. It's very satisfying not to waste anything. If you have some brown crabmeat, add that at the beginning.

Serves 4

extra virgin olive oil

shells and heads of 2 crabs

1 onion, roughly chopped

1 carrot, peeled and roughly chopped

1 celery stick, roughly chopped

2 garlic cloves, chopped

325ml white wine

4 tomatoes, chopped

1 tablespoon black peppercorns

a pinch of cayenne pepper

2 sprigs of thyme

a large pinch of saffron strands

3 star anise pods

2 bay leaves

zest of ½ orange

1 rounded tablespoon tomato purée

fish stock, to cover

100ml double cream

Beurre Manié (see page 70, tips), made with 15g soft unsalted butter and 15g plain flour (optional)

sea salt and black pepper

1 Heat a little oil in a large, heavy-based saucepan, add the crab shells and heads (along with any other fish heads and bones, if you have them) and cook until brown. Add the onion, carrot, celery and garlic and continue frying. Pour in the white wine, bring to the boil for 1 minute, then add the tomatoes, peppercorns, cayenne, thyme, saffron, star anise, bay leaves, orange zest, tomato purée and fish stock.

2 Bring to the boil, then simmer uncovered for 30 minutes, stirring occasionally. With a pair of tongs, remove the large shells, then strain the liquid through a sieve into a clean saucepan, pressing to extract the flavour from the final juices, which are the best. Add the cream and thicken with the *beurre manié*, whisking it into the soup a small piece at a time – you might not need it all. Simmer until the bisque thickens and season if necessary.

CRAB CAKES WITH RED PEPPER AND CUCUMBER SALSA

Crab cakes are delicious and I particularly love the way these ones are brightened up with lime and chilli.

Serves 4

400g potatoes, weighed after peeling

300g fresh white crabmeat

100g fresh brown crabmeat

1 egg yolk

2 tablespoons chopped coriander

finely grated zest of 1 lime

½ red chilli, finely chopped

plain flour for dusting

sunflower oil for shallow frying

3 eggs, lightly beaten

200g fine white breadcrumbs

sea salt and black pepper

For the salsa:

¼ cucumber, finely diced

¼ red onion, finely diced

¼ red pepper, finely diced

½ green chilli, finely diced

1 tomato, finely diced

2 tablespoons finely chopped chives

25ml rice wine vinegar

50ml olive oil

1 Boil the potatoes until soft, then drain well and mash. Put them in a large bowl with the crabmeat, egg yolk, coriander, lime zest and chilli, and season with salt and pepper. Shape the mixture into 8 cakes using a 5cm metal ring or pastry cutter, then dip them into the flour. Place on a tray, cover with cling film and put in the fridge to get cold and firm.

2 Meanwhile, make the salsa. Mix all the diced ingredients together in a colander, sprinkle with salt and leave to stand for 30 minutes to extract some of the liquid. Drain well, transfer to a bowl and add the chives, rice wine and olive oil, then season with salt and pepper. Set aside.

3 Heat 1cm of sunflower oil in a large non-stick frying pan. Put the beaten eggs and breadcrumbs in 2 separate bowls. Dip the crab cakes into the egg and then into the breadcrumbs. Place in the hot pan and cook for 3 minutes on each side. Serve with the salsa.

Preparing lobster

If you wish to cook a live lobster, first put it into a freezer for 2 hours, then bring a very large pan of well-salted water to the boil. If you are eating the lobster cold in a salad, cook it for 8 minutes from boiling. If it's going to be cooked further, boil it for just 5 minutes. These timings are for a 500–600g lobster and the bluish-grey shell will turn bright red during the boiling process. Set aside until cool enough to handle.

Take the cooled lobster and break off the large claws and the legs. Turn it on its back and use a large knife to cut through the shell and meat from the middle down to the tail, then from the middle to the head. Open out the shell into 2 separate halves. Pull out the bubble-like sac near the tail and the dark intestinal thread will come with it. Discard both. Remove the stomach sac, which looks like plastic and is near the head. Carefully scrape out the green tomalley, which is considered a delicacy, and freeze it to use in sauces or on pasta. Lift the meat out of the shell, rinse the shell halves and leave to drain.

Snap the large claw from its other 2 sections and break off the 'finger' under the claw. Crack the claw across the middle by tapping it with the sharp edge of a large knife, then slide off the shell. Repeat with the other claw. Crack the shell on the other sections of the claws and remove the meat. If possible, try to remove some meat from the legs in a similar way. Put the meat back into the drained lobster shells – the claw meat at the head end and the leg meat at the tail. The lobster is now ready to serve as you wish.

If you want to serve the lobster tail whole, simply pull off the head, then turn the lobster on its back and cut along the central line of the shell with a pair of kitchen scissors. Clean as described above, without removing the meat from the shell, then serve as you wish.

ROAST LOBSTER IN ITS SHELL

The smaller the lobster the sweeter, so try to buy ones that are 500–600g and that feel quite heavy for their size. Once you have prepared the lobsters, this is actually a very simple recipe. I love sucking the shells once I have devoured the flesh!

Serves 4

2 cooked lobsters, weighing about 500g each (see box opposite)

150g unsalted butter

4 tablespoons mixed chopped parsley, dill and chervil

sea salt and black pepper

1 Follow the instructions in the box opposite to prepare the lobster.

2 Melt the butter and pour it into the half lobsters. Sprinkle with the herbs and season with salt and pepper. Place in an oven preheated to 190°C/Gas Mark 5 and cook for 10 minutes, then serve with a herb salad.

LOBSTER SALAD WITH LITTLE GEM, TARRAGON AND CHERVIL

This is my version of a dish prepared for Queen Victoria. When the wonderful food historian Ivan Day told me about Victorian cooking, I was astonished how modern much of it was – and this recipe is a very good example. The only thing that has changed is the equipment we use.

Serves 4

2 cooked lobsters, weighing about 500g each (see page 195)

2 Little Gem lettuces, leaves separated

4 sprigs of tarragon, leaves removed

a small bunch of chervil

sea salt and black pepper

For the mayonnaise:

1 egg yolk

½ teaspoon Dijon mustard

150ml sunflower oil

½ teaspoon fine salt

2 teaspoons lemon juice

white pepper

For the vinaigrette:

1 teaspoon Dijon mustard

2 teaspoon white wine vinegar

50ml extra virgin olive oil

100ml sunflower oil

1 teaspoon sugar

1 Remove the meat from the lobsters (see page 195) and chop it into 2cm pieces.

2 Prepare a mayonnaise with the ingredients, as described on pages 157–158, steps 10–16, adding some white pepper too.

3 Put 4 tablespoons of the mayonnaise in a bowl. Add the lobster meat, mix well and season with salt and pepper.

4 Next, make the vinaigrette. Put the mustard and vinegar in a small bowl and whisk until thoroughly combined. Gradually pour in the 2 oils, whisking continuously. Add the sugar, then season with salt and pepper.

5 Chop the chervil, reserving some small sprigs for garnish. Add the lettuce and herbs to the vinaigrette and toss to coat. Put the leaves on to plates and top with a little lobster. Garnish with the reserved chervil.

Cleaning squid can be a messy job but it's surprisingly straightforward and you are left with lovely, pearly-white flesh afterwards. It's best cooked very quickly in a stir-fry to keep it succulent and tender.

SPICY SQUID

with basil and spinach

To clean the squid, follow steps 1 to 6

SERVES 4

4 medium squid, about 20cm long

2 tablespoons olive oil

1 tablespoon sesame oil

1 small shallot, thinly sliced

3 garlic cloves, very finely chopped

2cm piece of fresh ginger, finely chopped

1 teaspoon ground coriander

a pinch of saffron strands

1 small green chilli, finely chopped

30 basil leaves

sea salt and black pepper

FOR THE SPINACH:

30g unsalted butter

juice of 1 lemon

200g fresh spinach

1 To clean the squid, first pull the head away from the body.

2 Pull out the intestines – the ink sac, which is long and thin like a silver-blue fish, will probably come out too.

3 Remove the backbone, which looks like a piece of transparent plastic, and any of the remaining intestines.

4 Using a knife, scrape the thin brown skin off the flesh and rinse the body well inside and out.

5 Take the head and cut off the tentacles just in front of the eyes.

6 Discard the head.

7 Cut the tentacles to separate them. Rinse well.

8 Cut the wings off the body.

9 Score the wings with diamond shapes.

10 Cut the body into rings 5mm thick for this recipe, but leave whole if you are stuffing the squid.

11 Heat 1 tablespoon of the olive oil and the sesame oil in a small frying pan. Add the shallot, garlic and ginger and cook until softened.

12 Stir in the ground coriander, saffron and chilli.

13 Heat the remaining tablespoon of olive oil in a large frying pan, add the squid and fry over a high heat until lightly browned, about 1 minute.

14 Add the shallot mixture and cook over a high heat, stirring, for 30 seconds.

15 Season with salt and pepper, then toss in the basil leaves. Set aside while you cook the spinach.

16 Melt the butter with the lemon juice in a large frying pan, add the spinach and cook until wilted.

17 Drain well and gently press out all the excess liquid.

18 Toss with the squid and serve straight away.

TIPS AND IDEAS

■ When you buy squid, make sure it looks shiny and fresh, especially the eyes.

■ You can buy ready-cleaned squid, which is fine if that is all you can get, but it does mean you won't have the tentacles.

■ If the ink sac bursts when you are cleaning the squid, you will become covered in it, so be very careful. If you manage to remove it intact, you can freeze it and add to a fish soup, or use it to make fresh pasta (see page 244), substituting the ink for some of the egg.

■ Once you have prepared the squid, it freezes really well.

■ If you overcook squid it becomes tough – better to undercook it slightly rather than overcook it. Make sure the heat is high so it sears quickly.

■ Another wonderful cooking method for squid is to steam it. Squid rings will take about 3 minutes. As with frying, be careful not to overcook it or it will become tough and chewy.

■ Fast cooking is the rule with squid when frying, grilling or steaming, but it can also be braised, in which case longer, slower cooking is needed.

spicy squid variations

Chinese-style Spicy Squid – prepare 2 medium squid as described on page 199, steps 1–10. Heat 2 tablespoons sesame oil in a large frying pan and quickly cook the squid in it until lightly browned. Remove from the pan and set aside. Add 1 finely sliced onion to the pan, along with 100g mangetout, 100g baby corn, 100g shiitake mushrooms, 2 finely chopped garlic cloves, 1 tablespoon finely chopped fresh ginger and 1 teaspoon finely chopped chilli and stir-fry until *al dente*. Mix 1 teaspoon cornflour to a paste with 2 teaspoons water. Add to the pan with 1 tablespoon soy sauce and cook for 1 minute. Return the squid to the pan, heat through briefly and serve straight away.

Spicy Squid with Chorizo and Spinach – prepare the squid as described on page 199, steps 1–10. Heat 2 tablespoons olive oil in a large frying pan, quickly cook the squid in it until lightly browned, then remove and set aside. Fry 1 finely sliced shallot, 3 very finely chopped garlic cloves and 1 finely chopped green chilli in the oil until soft, then add 200g chopped cooking chorizo and fry until lightly browned. Return the squid to the pan, add 200g fresh spinach and cook briefly until wilted. Add a handful of chopped coriander and serve immediately.

CALAMARI WITH LEMON CRÈME FRAÎCHE DIP

Two squid would probably be sufficient here rather than four but this dish is always so popular that I tend to make it in large quantities.

Serves 4

200g plain flour
1 tablespoon chopped coriander
½ teaspoon cayenne pepper
4 medium squid, cleaned and cut into rings (see page 199, steps 1–10)
sunflower oil for deep-frying
1 lemon, cut into wedges, to serve
sea salt and black pepper

For the crème fraîche dip:

200g crème fraîche
1 garlic clove, finely crushed
juice and grated zest of ½ lemon
2 tablespoons chopped dill
a pinch of cayenne pepper

1 First put all the dip ingredients into a bowl, season with salt and pepper and mix well.

2 Put the flour, coriander and cayenne into a bowl, season with salt and pepper, then toss in the squid rings and all the tentacles. Heat some oil in a deep-fat fryer or large, deep saucepan to 190°C, then cook the squid in batches for 2–3 minutes, until golden brown. Drain on kitchen paper. Serve with the dip and wedges of lemon on the side.

STUFFED BABY SQUID WITH BASIL DRESSING

This lovely dish goes very well with couscous. The stuffing expands quite a lot during cooking, so be careful not to overfill the squid.

Serves 4

12 baby squid, cleaned (see page 199, steps 1–7)

300g raw tiger prawns, peeled and deveined (see page 212, step 1)

4 tablespoons chopped mixed dill and parsley

1 egg yolk

100g ricotta cheese

mizuna leaves

sea salt and black pepper

½ red pepper, deseeded and finely diced, to garnish

For the basil dressing:

a large handful of basil

100ml olive oil

juice of ½ lemon

sea salt and black pepper

1 Finely chop the squid tentacles and the prawns. Put them into a bowl, add the herbs, egg yolk and ricotta, season with salt and pepper and mix well.

2 Half-fill each squid body sac with the ricotta mixture. Wrap them in cling film.

3 To make the dressing, put all the ingredients in a blender and blitz to a purée.

4 Set a steamer over a saucepan of simmering water, add the wrapped squid and steam for 3–5 minutes; it should be slightly springy to the touch. Discard the cling film. Put a few mizuna leaves on each plate, then place 3 stuffed squid on top. Garnish with diced red pepper and pour a little basil dressing over the top.

DEEP-FRIED SQUID WITH SWEET SESAME DIPPING SAUCE

Deep-frying squid is my favourite way of serving it, and the combination of flavours here is unbeatable.

Serves 4

100g plain flour

2 eggs, beaten

250g fine white breadcrumbs

4 squid, cleaned and cut into rings (see page 199, steps 1–10)

sunflower oil for deep-frying

sea salt and black pepper

For the sweet sesame dipping sauce:

2 tablespoons caster sugar

½ red chilli, finely chopped

2 spring onions, finely chopped

1 garlic clove, finely chopped

1 tablespoon finely chopped fresh ginger

2 tablespoons finely chopped coriander

juice and grated zest of 1 lime

2 tablespoons soy sauce

2 tablespoons sesame oil

2 tablespoons Chinese rice vinegar

1 teaspoon tomato purée

1 First make the dipping sauce. Put all the ingredients into a small bowl and mix well. Set aside until required.

2 Put the flour in a bowl and season with salt and pepper. Put the eggs and the breadcrumbs in 2 separate bowls. Toss the squid rings and tentacles in the flour, shake off the excess, then dip in the egg and toss in the breadcrumbs.

3 Heat 5cm of oil in a deep-fat fryer or large, deep saucepan to 190°C. Fry the squid in batches for 2–3 minutes, until golden brown, then drain on kitchen paper and keep warm. Serve with the sweet sesame dipping sauce.

SHELLFISH

203

My first serious introduction to scallops was when I worked in the Hebrides and had to prepare hundreds at a time. I was shown this very clever way of removing them from their shells by a fisherman there and have followed his method ever since. Serve this dish as a starter or a main course.

SCALLOPS EN PAPILLOTE

with curried coconut milk and pak choi

To prepare the scallops, follow steps 1 to 7

SERVES 4

8 scallops in the shell

4 tablespoons olive oil

2 heads of pak choi, cut lengthways into quarters

12 mangetout, cut lengthways into fine strips

½ red pepper, skinned (see page 32, step 1), deseeded and cut into fine strips

4 spring onions, cut into fine strips

sea salt and black pepper

FOR THE SAUCE:

½ red pepper, skinned (see page 32, step 1), deseeded and chopped

½ green pepper, deseeded and chopped

1 small red chilli, chopped

1 small shallot, chopped

1 garlic clove, chopped

2cm piece of fresh ginger, grated

2 teaspoons ground cumin

4 seeds from a green cardamom pod

1 teaspoon turmeric

2 teaspoons caster sugar

2 tablespoons olive oil

juice of 1 lemon

250ml coconut milk

1 Stand a scallop, hinge-end up, on a chopping board with the flat-shell side facing away from you. Insert a sharp, flexible knife between the shells.

2 Run the knife from the hinge to the bottom of the shell, scraping hard against the flat side. The shell will automatically spring open.

3 Remove and discard the 'skirt' from around the scallop.

4 Run your flexible knife under the scallop muscle and cut against the shell – there is only a 1cm-wide piece of gristle holding the muscle.

5 Discard the muscle and the black intestines surrounding it.

6 Rinse the scallop carefully under cold gently running water as it is quite delicate.

7 Remove the orange roe and the thin skin surrounding it. Reserve the roe for using in salads, sauces or terrines and discard the skin. Repeat with the remaining scallops.

8 Place the prepared scallops on a tray lined with a clean, dry cloth, cover and refrigerate until you are ready to cook them.

9 To make the sauce, put the peppers, chilli, shallot, garlic and ginger into a food processor and whiz to a purée.

10 Transfer to a small frying pan and add all the spices, the sugar and oil. Cook gently for about 15 minutes, stirring often.

11 Stir in the lemon juice and coconut milk and simmer for 2 minutes. Turn off the heat and leave for a couple of hours to infuse (this can be done the night before).

12 Bring the sauce to the boil, then reduce the heat and simmer until it starts to thicken.

13 Strain the sauce through a fine sieve and season with salt and pepper.

14 Heat 2 tablespoons of the olive oil in a large frying pan, add the pak choi and cook for 5–10 minutes, until softened, turning often.

15 Remove from the pan and drain on kitchen paper.

16 Put the scallops into a bowl, add the remaining 2 tablespoons oil and toss to coat. Season with salt and pepper.

17 Heat a dry frying pan until quite hot. Add the scallops and cook for about 30 seconds, until browned, on each side.

18 Remove from the pan and leave to rest for 2 minutes.

19 Cut 4 large circles about 38cm in diameter out of greaseproof paper.

20 Divide the pak choi equally between the paper circles, then add the mangetout strips and season with salt and pepper.

21 Top with 2 scallops per circle, then sprinkle over the red pepper and spring onions.

22 Add 2 tablespoons of the sauce to each circle, then fold up the paper, crimping it over the top to seal. Reserve the remaining sauce.

23 Put the paper parcels on baking trays and place in an oven preheated to 180°C/Gas Mark 4, then cook for 8–10 minutes.

24 Transfer each parcel directly to a serving plate, open each one and pour over a little more sauce before serving.

scallop variations

Scallops with Cream and Vermouth Sauce – prepare the scallops following the instructions on page 205, steps 1–7. Put the scallop 'skirts' in a pan with 300ml double cream and 2 tablespoons vermouth and bring to the boil. Simmer until reduced by half, then season with salt and white pepper and strain. Sear the scallops as described on page 206, steps 16– 17, this time cooking them for about 30 seconds on each side. Serve with the sauce.

Scallops with Courgettes – prepare the scallops following the instructions on page 205, steps 1–7. Then sear the scallops as described on page 206, steps 16– 17, cooking them for about 30 seconds on each side. Serve with Ribbon Courgettes (see page 33).

Scallops with Sauce Vierge – prepare the scallops following the instructions on page 205, steps 1–7. Then sear the scallops as described on page 206, steps 16– 17, cooking them for about 30 seconds on each side. Serve with Sauce Vierge (see page 162).

TIPS AND IDEAS

■ Buying scallops in the shell means that they are really fresh. Ready-prepared ones have often been previously frozen. You should be able to get them in the shell if you order them in advance from your fishmonger.

■ If a scallop is off, you will know immediately by the very bad smell when you open it up.

■ When searing scallops, always oil them rather than the pan, and make sure the pan is hot before you add them.

■ Scallops should never be cooked for long, or they will be as tough as old boots. They should be soft and succulent in the centre.

■ I don't tend to cook the coral with the scallops, although a lot of people like to – it's purely a matter of preference, so leave them attached if you prefer.

■ The frilly 'skirt' around the scallop is well worth saving for sauces. Only the skirt, the muscle and the coral are edible – discard everything else.

■ It's fun to have the shells. You can scrub them clean, line them with puff pastry and bake them to make attractive pastry 'containers' that can be filled as you wish.

COQUILLES ST JACQUES

If you are lucky enough to have fresh, unopened scallops, there is nothing nicer than presenting them in the shells. If you don't have the shells, serve them in little 'eared' dishes instead with Creamed Potatoes (see page 86).

Serves 4

8 large scallops in their shells, cleaned (see page 205, steps 1–7), roes and shells reserved

2 tablespoons olive oil

75g unsalted butter

120g button mushrooms, sliced

300ml fish stock

150ml white wine

1 small onion, very finely chopped

15g plain flour

150ml double cream

1 tablespoon finely chopped curly parsley

2 egg yolks

4 tablespoons fresh breadcrumbs

4 tablespoons freshly grated Parmesan cheese

4 tablespoons grated Gruyère cheese

sea salt and white pepper

1 Put the scallops into a bowl, add the oil and season with salt and white pepper. Heat a dry frying pan, add the scallops and lightly brown on each side. This should take no more than 30 seconds per side. Set aside to rest.

2 In the same frying pan, melt 30g of the butter, add the mushrooms and cook for about 3 minutes. Stir in 2 tablespoons of the fish stock.

3 Put the wine in a saucepan, bring to the boil and simmer until reduced by half. Melt the remaining 45g butter in another small saucepan, add the onion and cook until softened. Add the flour and stir to make a paste, then gradually add the reduced wine, the remaining fish stock and any juices from the scallops, stirring continuously. Simmer for about 3 minutes, then add the cream. Simmer again and season with salt and white pepper, then add the parsley. Once the mixture has thickened slightly, allow to cool a little, then fold in the egg yolks.

4 Put a scallop in each cleaned scallop shell and sprinkle the mushrooms around. Pour some sauce over each scallop, then place the shells on a baking tray. Mix the breadcrumbs, Parmesan and Gruyère in a bowl and season with salt and white pepper. Sprinkle the mixture over the scallops and mushrooms. Place in an oven preheated to 180°C/ Gas Mark 4 and cook for 10 minutes, until pale golden. Serve immediately.

MUSSELS ST JEAN

A little curry powder works well with mussels. Serve as a starter, with crusty bread.

Serves 4

1.5kg mussels

400ml white wine

50g unsalted butter

35g plain flour

600ml milk

1 rounded tablespoon medium-hot curry powder

150ml double cream

2 tablespoons chopped curly parsley

sea salt and black pepper

1 First clean the mussels if they have not already been cleaned (see box).

2 Put the wine into a large saucepan and bring it to the boil. Add the mussels, cover with a lid and cook, shaking the pan, until all the shells have opened. Discard any that do not open. Remove the mussels and strain through a sieve lined with fine muslin, reserving the liquid. Now remove and discard the top shell of each mussel.

3 Wipe out the saucepan, melt the butter in it, then add the flour and stir to make a smooth paste. Pour in the milk gradually, stirring constantly, until it starts to simmer. Now add the curry powder, half the mussel liquid and the cream. Bring to the boil and whisk well. Season with salt and pepper and add the mussels. Pour into a large dish and sprinkle the parsley on top.

POTTED SHRIMP

Shrimps are always sold cooked and with the shells on, so you have to go through the lengthy process of taking them off – a tedious job but I rather enjoy it. Shrimps are such a treat, and this recipe can be prepared well in advance. It also freezes well.

Serves 4

600g brown shrimp with shells (400g peeled weight)

130g salted butter

¼ teaspoon cayenne pepper

½ teaspoon black pepper

¼ teaspoon freshly grated nutmeg

sea salt

lemon wedges, to serve

1 Peel the shrimp and discard the shells. Melt the butter in a small saucepan, add the cayenne, black pepper and nutmeg, then add the shrimp and stir well. Season with salt, but not too much. Put into 4 ramekins and pack the shrimps down tightly. Top with a little more butter to create a thin layer on top. Put into the fridge for 4 hours.

2 Serve with lemon wedges and good brown bread.

Cleaning mussels and clams

First pull off the beards, which are the brown fibrous threads hanging from the shells. Using a knife, scrape off any barnacles attached to the shell. Give the mussels or clams a rinse in lots of cold water. If they are slightly open, tap them sharply on a surface and if they do not close, discard them. Rinse again and they are ready to cook. Discard any that do not open during cooking.

SPICY TIGER PRAWNS WITH POTATO AND CAPER SALAD

Potatoes go extremely well with prawns (and, indeed, with lobsters and langoustines). The contrasting textures just seem to work. These prawns are delicious served at room temperature.

Serves 4

20 raw tiger prawns in their shells

olive oil

cress, to garnish

For the marinade:

½ onion, finely chopped

6 garlic cloves, finely chopped

2cm piece of fresh ginger, finely chopped

1 red chilli, chopped

2 teaspoons sugar

1 teaspoon ground cumin

1 tablespoon ground coriander

6 tablespoons olive oil

For the potato and caper salad:

16 small new potatoes

1 egg yolk

¼ tablespoon Dijon mustard

150ml olive oil

5 basil leaves, cut into thin strips

2 tablespoons finely chopped curly parsley

15g capers, chopped

sea salt and white pepper

1 First prepare the prawns. Remove the heads and carefully peel off all the shell. You can use the heads and shells to make stock, if you like. Using the tip of a sharp knife, cut along the top of the prawns and remove the dark intestinal tract (this is known as deveining). Cut three-quarters of the way through the prawns lengthways and open out the flesh (this is known as butterflying).

2 To make the marinade, place all the ingredients in a food processor and blitz to a purée. Mix with the prawns, then cover and leave to marinate in the fridge for at least 2 hours, but preferably overnight.

3 To make the salad, bring a pan of water to the boil, add the potatoes and cook until tender. Be careful not to overcook them. Set aside until cool enough to handle, then remove the skins.

4 Make a mayonnaise with the egg yolk, mustard and oil as described on page 157, steps 10–17. Season with salt and white pepper. Add the basil, parsley and chopped capers and check the seasoning again. Cut the potatoes in half and stir them into the mayonnaise.

5 Heat some oil in a large frying pan over a medium-high heat, add the prawns in batches and cook until browned – about 1 minute on each side. Be careful not to overcrowd the pan or they will braise. Serve the prawns with the potato and caper salad and garnish with cress.

THAI WHITE FISH AND PRAWN CURRY

Serves 4

2 tablespoons groundnut oil

1 onion, chopped

2 garlic cloves, chopped

2.5cm piece of fresh ginger, finely chopped

300ml fish stock

400ml coconut milk

2 teaspoons Thai fish sauce

3 kaffir lime leaves

1 teaspoon light brown sugar

2 lemongrass stalks, halved lengthways

700g white fish fillets, skinned and cut into bite-sized pieces

20 raw tiger prawns, peeled and deveined (see opposite, step 1)

150ml double cream

6 sprigs of coriander, chopped

6 large basil leaves, finely shredded

sea salt and black pepper

For the hot paste:

7 long red chillies

2 tablespoons chopped lemongrass

1 tablespoon chopped fresh ginger

2 tablespoons chopped shallots

1 tablespoon chopped garlic

1 tablespoon turmeric

For the fragrant rice:

½ teaspoon caraway seeds

4 whole cloves

6 cardamom pods

2 bay leaves

500ml vegetable stock

350g basmati rice, rinsed

For the pak choi:

2 tablespoons olive oil

2 heads of pak choi, chopped

½ red bird's eye chilli, finely chopped

1 First, make the hot paste. Deseed the chillies, then place in a blender with the other ingredients and a little water and blitz until smooth. Set aside.

2 Heat the groundnut oil in a large saucepan, add the onion, garlic and ginger and cook over a low heat for 4–5 minutes, until softened and translucent. Stir in 1–2 tablespoons of the hot paste and cook for a further minute. Add the fish stock, coconut milk, fish sauce, lime leaves, sugar and lemongrass stalks and bring to the boil. Simmer gently for 20–25 minutes, then remove and discard the lemongrass.

3 Meanwhile, make the fragrant rice. Place the caraway seeds, cloves, cardamom pods and bay leaves in a square of muslin, bring the corners together and secure with a piece of string. Place the spice parcel in a large saucepan with the vegetable stock and a pinch of salt. Bring to the boil, then simmer for 10 minutes so that the flavours infuse. Discard the parcel. Put the rice in a separate pan and pour enough of the infused stock to come about 1cm above the rice. Bring to a simmer, cover with a tight-fitting lid and cook for 10 minutes. Turn off the heat and leave, untouched, for 5 minutes. Remove the lid and gently fluff up the rice with a fork.

4 For the pak choi, heat the oil in a frying pan, add the pak choi and chilli and cook for a few minutes, stirring frequently. Season with salt and pepper.

5 Add the fish and prawns to the coconut mixture, then bring to the boil and simmer for 4–6 minutes. Add the cream, coriander and basil leaves and season with salt and pepper. Serve with the pak choi, spooned over bowls of fragrant rice.

SAUTÉED CHILLI PRAWNS

This is a wonderful, decorative dish.

Serves 4

20 raw tiger prawns, peeled, deveined and butterflied (see page 212, step 1)

1 red chilli, very finely chopped

olive oil

1 tablespoon hoisin sauce

1 tablespoon soy sauce

2cm piece of fresh ginger, very finely chopped

2 garlic cloves, very finely chopped

1 red pepper, skinned (see page 32, step 1), deseeded and cut into fine strips

sea salt and black pepper

basil leaves, to garnish

For the roast tomatoes:

12 baby vine tomatoes

juice of ½ lemon

½ teaspoon salt

1 teaspoon black pepper

2 teaspoons thyme leaves

1 tablespoon sugar

1 First make the tomatoes. Put them into a baking dish with the other ingredients. Place in an oven preheated to 180°C/Gas Mark 4 and cook for 15–20 minutes, until the skins start to split and peel off.

2 Put the prawns into a large bowl, add the chilli and season with salt and pepper. Heat some oil in a large frying pan, add the prawns and stir-fry quickly until just cooked through. Transfer to a bowl.

3 In the same pan, add the hoisin sauce, soy sauce, ginger, garlic and a dash of water, bring to the boil and reduce to thick syrup. Add the red pepper and the cooked prawns. Continue cooking for 1 minute. Serve the prawns with the roasted tomatoes and garnish with basil leaves.

PRAWN COCKTAIL

I don't think you can beat a really good homemade prawn cocktail. This one includes grapefruit, which goes so well with seafood.

Serves 4

1 grapefruit, peeled and segmented (see page 41, step 27)

16 raw tiger prawns, peeled and deveined (see page 212, step 1)

1 Little Gem lettuce, shredded

1 teaspoon extra virgin olive oil

sea salt and black pepper

paprika for dusting

micro herbs or small salad leaves, to garnish

For the sauce:

1 egg yolk

½ teaspoon Dijon mustard

150ml sunflower oil

juice of ¼ lemon

1 tablespoon tomato ketchup

a few drops of Tabasco sauce

sea salt

1 First make the sauce. Whisk the egg yolk and mustard together, then add the oil very slowly, drop by drop at first, whisking constantly. Season with salt and beat in the lemon juice, then add the ketchup and Tabasco.

2 Cut the grapefruit segments into 6. Put the prawns in a steamer over a pan of simmering water and cook for 3 minutes, until just cooked through. Allow to cool and reserve 4 for garnish. Cut the remaining prawns in half lengthways and fold into the sauce with the grapefruit.

3 Put the lettuce in a bowl. Add the olive oil and toss, then season with salt and pepper.

4 To serve, divide the lettuce between 4 glasses and top with the prawn mixture. Garnish each with a whole prawn and a few micro herbs or small salad leaves and dust with a little paprika.

1 First put the tomatoes, leek, celery, carrot, parsley, garlic and thyme into a food processor and blitz until finely chopped.

2 Transfer to a bowl and add the egg whites and minced beef. Mix together thoroughly.

3 Add the mixture to the cold beef stock in a large saucepan – this looks disgusting, but don't worry because it will soon turn into a clear consommé.

4 Bring to the boil, stirring constantly.

5 Reduce the heat and simmer for about 1 hour. Do not stir, and don't let it boil again, otherwise the consommé could become cloudy.

6 The meat and the vegetables will rise to the top, forming a crust. Make a hole in the crust with the back of a ladle to allow the steam to come out.

7 Turn off the heat and leave to stand for 30 minutes. Using the back of the ladle again, enlarge the hole in the crust.

8 Strain the stock through a sieve lined with a double layer of fine muslin into a clean pan, being very careful not to pour too quickly.

9 Season with salt and gently warm through to serve.

TIPS AND IDEAS

■ It's essential to use good homemade stock for consommé.

■ I like to add some chopped vegetables with the meat and egg whites. These are purely for flavour and could be omitted if you prefer.

■ Resist the temptation to stir the consommé after it has come to the boil, or it will be cloudy rather than clear.

■ Leaving the consommé to stand after cooking allows it to settle and the crust to firm up slightly.

■ You need to add quite a lot of salt to consommé to bring out the flavour. Taste it after straining and season as necessary.

■ If the stock doesn't become clear, you can rescue it by clarifying it a second time, using just egg whites mixed with their broken-up shells.

GAME CONSOMMÉ

Game gives consommé a really deep, earthy flavour. All you need to garnish is a little chopped parsley.

Serves 4

2 litres cold game stock

4 tablespoons sherry (optional)

sea salt and white pepper

chopped parsley, to garnish

For the clarification:

1 celery stick, roughly chopped

1 leek, roughly chopped

1 carrot, peeled and roughly chopped

4 tomatoes, roughly chopped

a handful of mixed tarragon, parsley and chervil leaves

1 chicken breast, skinned and boned

5 egg whites

1 To make the clarification, put the vegetables into a food processor with the tomatoes, herbs and chicken breast, process well, then place in a large pan with the egg whites and 2 tablespoons water.

2 Add the cold stock and stir well. Bring to a simmer slowly, stirring all the time. When you see the first bubbles, turn the heat down to a very gentle simmer and do not stir any more. Continue simmering gently for about 1 hour, then turn off the heat off and leave to stand for 30 minutes.

3 Carefully pour the liquid through a fine-meshed sieve lined with muslin and set over a large bowl. Be careful not to move the vegetables around too much or the liquid will become cloudy. Season well with salt and white pepper.

4 To serve, heat the consommé in a pan, pour it into soup bowls and add 1 tablespoon sherry, if using, to each bowl. Garnish with the parsley.

CHICKEN CONSOMMÉ WITH BREAD AND PARSLEY DUMPLINGS

This chicken consommé dish is a real pick-me-up if you're feeling a bit fragile. The dumplings are particularly light and warming.

Serves 4

2 litres cold chicken stock

finely chopped chives, to garnish

sea salt and black pepper

For the clarification:

100g tomatoes, chopped

100g celery, chopped

100g carrots, peeled and chopped

4 sprigs of tarragon

2 sprigs of parsley

5 egg whites

200g minced chicken

For the bread and parsley dumplings:

150g fresh white breadcrumbs

1 teaspoon bicarbonate of soda

3 tablespoons hot water

1 egg

3 tablespoons chopped parsley

a pinch of cayenne pepper

1 First prepare the clarification as instructed on page 219, steps 1 and 2. Add it to 1.5 litres of the chicken stock and follow steps 3–8 on page 219. Season with salt and pepper.

2 To make the dumplings, put all the ingredients into a food processor, season with salt and blitz well until clumping together. Form into marble-sized balls.

3 Bring the remaining stock to a low simmer in a saucepan. Drop the dumplings into the stock and cook for about 15 minutes. Remove from the pan and leave to cool.

4 To serve, gently warm the chicken consommé, then carefully add the dumplings one by one so that they don't break up, then warm through. Gently ladle into bowls and garnish with finely chopped chives.

chicken consommé variation

Beetroot Consommé – follow the recipe above to make the chicken consommé but add 300g peeled and chopped raw beetroot to the other ingredients for the clarification. This will give the consommé a vibrant red colour.

SEAFOOD CONSOMMÉ

This recipe sounds very luxurious but it's surprisingly thrifty to make, as you need only a little white fish besides the shells. People tend to throw away the shells of seafood but they are full of flavour. Give your fishmonger notice that you will need some – I'm sure they will oblige. Otherwise, you can save up shells in your freezer until you have enough.

Serves 4

a drizzle of olive oil

1kg seafood shells, such as crab, lobster and/ or prawns

½ fennel bulb, chopped

1 onion, chopped

1 carrot, peeled and chopped

a few sprigs of parsley

250ml white wine

a pinch of saffron strands

3 litres fish stock

2 tablespoons tomato purée

sea salt and black pepper

For the clarification:

250g skinned, lean white fish fillets, such as whiting or cod

100g carrots, peeled and chopped

1 small leek, white part only

3 sprigs of parsley

3 sprigs of tarragon or 2 teaspoons dried tarragon

2 garlic cloves, chopped

a good pinch of saffron strands

5 egg whites

1 Heat the oil in a large, flameproof casserole, add the seafood shells and cook for a few minutes. Add the fennel, onion, carrot and parsley and cook until browned. Add the wine and saffron and simmer for 5 minutes, until reduced. Stir in the fish stock and tomato purée, bring to the boil, then reduce the heat and simmer for 20 minutes. Strain through a fine sieve and leave to cool completely.

2 For the clarification, put the fish, carrots, leek, parsley, tarragon, garlic and saffron in a food processor and blitz to a purée. Transfer to a bowl and add the egg whites. Mix together very well.

3 Pour the cold fish stock into a large saucepan. Add the clarification, then follow the instructions on page 219, steps 4–8, but simmer the consommé for 20–25 minutes and leave to stand for 15 minutes before straining, carefully ladling the consommé through a colander lined with a double layer of muslin into a clean pan. Season with salt and pepper and gently warm through to serve.

TOMATO AND VODKA CONSOMMÉ JELLY WITH CRAB AND PRAWNS

This is a little different from the other recipes in this chapter as it is not derived from a meat or fish stock, but the principle of concentrating the flavour of the tomatoes is the same. Make this only at the peak of the tomato season, as you need to use tomatoes that are ripe, juicy and flavourful. The result is a very soft jelly that barely holds its shape, full of the taste of summer.

Serves 4

2½kg very ripe tomatoes

a handful of basi

100ml vodka

1 teaspoon tomato purée

about 1½ gelatine leaves

sea salt and black pepper

2 tomatoes, skinned (see page 278, step 1), deseeded and cut into strips, to garnish

pea shoots, to garnish

For the crab and prawns:

4 large crab claws, cooked

4 raw prawns in their shells

1–2 tablespoons crème fraîche

1–2 teaspoons lemon juice

1 Put the tomatoes, basil, vodka and tomato purée into a blender in batches and blitz until smooth. Transfer to a large sieve lined with fine muslin set over a large bowl. Leave overnight.

2 The next day, measure the juice that has collected in the bowl and for every 500ml, use 1 gelatine leaf. Soak the gelatine in a bowl of cold water for 10 minutes, then drain and squeeze out the water. Leave in the bowl. Warm some of the tomato juice in a saucepan, season with salt and pepper and add to the gelatine. When the gelatine has melted, add it to the bowl of juice. Stir well, then transfer it to a shallow dish and leave in the fridge for 3 hours to set.

3 To prepare the crab and prawns, take all the meat out of the crab claws as instructed on page 189, steps 11–12. Put the prawns in the top of a steamer and steam for 2–3 minutes, until they turn pink. Leave until cool enough to handle, then peel and devein them (see page 212, step 1). Cut the prawns into pieces. Mix with the crabmeat, crème fraîche and lemon juice to taste, season with salt and pepper and toss gently.

4 To serve, put a 5cm metal ring or pastry cutter in the centre of each soup plate and fill with the crab mixture. Remove the ring, then garnish the mounds with pea shoots. Spoon some lightly set jelly around each mound and garnish with the tomato strips.

CONFIT

Confit is a cooking term that can apply to
various types of preserve, but is often used to
refer to meat cooked very slowly in fat and then
stored in it. It's been around for centuries but is
currently enjoying a revival as people rediscover
the amazing flavours that can develop. Confit of
duck is well known but you can also apply the
technique to other meats, fish and even fruits and
vegetables. Once you have your confit, you can go
on to use it in so many ways: in pies, pâtés and
casseroles, in salads, coated in breadcrumbs and
fried, or as a garnish.

Confit of duck works well with sweet accompaniments.
This recipe uses rosehip syrup and is absolutely delicious.

CONFIT OF DUCK

and warm summer bean salad with tarragon and rosehip

To prepare the confit of duck, follow steps 1 to 7

SERVES 4

4 large duck legs

200g coarse sea salt

30g white peppercorns, crushed

a bunch of thyme sprigs

6 garlic cloves, crushed

1kg duck or goose fat

4 tablespoons rosehip syrup

FOR THE SUMMER BEAN SALAD:

1kg broad beans in their pods (300g shelled weight)

600g peas in their pods (150g shelled weight)

2 tomatoes, skinned (see page 278, step 1), deseeded and finely diced

2 tablespoons roughly chopped tarragon

50ml olive oil

1 tablespoon lemon juice

1 teaspoon clear honey

12 asparagus spears, trimmed

sea salt and black pepper

1 First prepare your duck legs. Using a meat cleaver or a sharp, heavy knife, cut off the knuckles from the drumsticks.

2 Place the legs, skin-side down, in a deep dish. Sprinkle over the coarse salt, crushed peppercorns, thyme and garlic, then rub into the legs a little.

3 Cover and leave in the fridge overnight to draw the liquid out of the meat.

4 Remove the dish from the fridge, wipe the salt off the duck legs and pat dry.

5 In a heavy-based flameproof casserole, heat the duck or goose fat to a simmer, then remove from the heat, add the duck legs and cover.

6 Place the dish in an oven preheated to 150°C/Gas Mark 2 and cook, covered, for 2½–3 hours, until very tender. Remove from the oven.

7 Lift the legs out of the fat and drain well. If not using straight away, leave to cool completely, then cover and keep in the fridge for up to 1 week.

8 For the salad, first shell all the beans and peas, then cook separately in boiling water for 1 minute.

9 Drain, refresh in a bowl of iced water and drain again.

10 Peel the broad beans and discard the skins.

11 Put the beans into a bowl with the peas, tomatoes and tarragon.

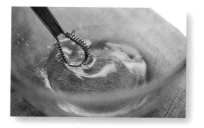

12 Whisk together the oil, lemon juice and honey, then season with salt and pepper.

CONFIT

229

13 Add the dressing to the vegetables and toss to coat thoroughly.

14 Cut the asparagus spears in half at an angle. Cook in boiling water for 30 seconds.

15 Drain the asparagus, refresh under cold running water and drain again. Add to the vegetable mixture.

16 Put the prepared duck legs into a roasting tin and brush the rosehip syrup all over them.

17 Place in an oven preheated to 190°C/Gas Mark 5 and roast for 10–15 minutes, until crispy.

18 Meanwhile, heat the vegetables gently until warm, then serve them with the confit of duck, sprinkled with the duck pan juices.

TIPS AND IDEAS

■ If you buy a whole duck, you can take the breasts off to cook separately, then use the carcass for stock and the legs for confit.

■ Before marinating the legs, you could remove the thigh bone (without cutting the meat open – just dig carefully round the bone with your knife), leaving the drumstick in. This makes neater finished legs if you are serving them whole, and also means that if you preserve them in fat, you can pack them into the jar more easily.

■ If you cannot get goose or duck fat, use 1 litre of olive oil instead.

■ The meat should be very tender indeed after cooking. If it flakes away from the bone easily when teased with a fork, it is done.

■ When making fish confit, you really do need a temperature probe.

■ It's almost impossible to overcook confit, so don't worry about timing it precisely – the important thing is not to undercook it.

■ The fat can be strained and used again – for confit or for roast potatoes.

■ Once you have cooked the duck legs, you can preserve them by putting them into a very large, sterilised Kilner jar (see page 21), pouring over the goose or duck fat, making sure the legs are completely immersed in it, and sealing the jar. This is the traditional way of storing them and they will keep for months in a cool, dark place. Once you open the jar, you will need to use the confit within 6 days.

■ The confit meat is best served hot, so always sear it in a hot pan or in a roasting tin, either on or off the bone, to crisp it up. Cut the skin into strips or dice and fry that too for a garnish.

confit of duck variations

Confit of Chicken or Goose Legs – follow steps 1–7 of the recipe on pages 228–229, replacing the duck legs with chicken or goose legs and reducing the cooking time to about 2 hours for chicken legs.

Confit of Duck with Honey and Soy – follow steps 1–7 of the recipe on pages 228–229. Then mix together 2 tablespoons each of honey, brown sugar and soy sauce and brush over the duck legs before crisping them up in the oven (see page 230, steps 16–17). They are delicious served with pineapple, and this is one of the few occasions when I would use tinned fruit. Put the pineapple slices in the roasting tin under the meat.

Confit of Duck with Hoisin Sauce – follow steps 1–7 of the recipe on pages 228–229 . Then take the confit duck meat off the bone and sear in a frying pan to crisp it up. Serve wrapped in iceberg lettuce leaves, accompanied by hoisin sauce.

Confit of Duck in Filo – follow steps 1–7 of the recipe on pages 228–229. Then take the confit duck meat off the bone, wrap in filo pastry to make little parcels and brush with olive oil. Bake at 180°C/Gas Mark 4 until the pastry is golden and the duck is thoroughly heated through.

Confit of Duck with Juniper Berries – follow steps 1–7 of the recipe on pages 228–229, adding 1 tablespoon lightly crushed juniper berries to the salt mixture.

CONFIT OF DUCK WITH A QUICK CASSOULET

This is a cheat's cassoulet, and you can pretty much assemble it from the storecupboard, as long as you have some confit of duck tucked away.

Serves 4

4 large pork sausages

1 tablespoon duck fat

4 confit duck legs (see pages 228–229, steps 1–7)

150g piece of smoked bacon, cut into 1cm pieces

100g onion, finely chopped

530g cooked haricot beans, drained

4 garlic cloves, finely chopped

800ml chicken stock

4 tomatoes, skinned (see page 278, step 1), deseeded and chopped

2 carrots, sliced

4 bay leaves

bouquet garni

4 sprigs of thyme

1 tablespoon tomato purée

sea salt and black pepper

1 Cut the sausages into 2cm pieces. Heat a little of the duck fat in a flameproof casserole over a medium heat, add the sausages and cook until browned on all sides. Remove and set aside.

2 Add the confit duck legs to the casserole and cook until browned all over. Remove and set aside. Add a little more duck fat to the casserole and gently brown the bacon in it. Add the onion and cook until softened but not browned.

3 Add the haricot beans, garlic, stock, tomatoes, carrots, bay leaves, bouquet garni and thyme and bring to a simmer. Add the tomato purée and the sausages. Cut through the duck legs to separate the thighs and drumsticks and add to the cassoulet. Place in an oven preheated to 180°C/Gas Mark 4 and cook for about 45 minutes. Remove, season with salt and pepper and serve.

CONFIT OF BELLY PORK WITH KALE

Confit of pork is not as well known as confit of duck but it's a wonderful way to prepare pork, and it keeps for 4–5 days in the fridge. You can confit the meat well in advance and finish the dish just before serving. You could also wrap the confit of belly pork in foil, carve the joint into steak-like portions and then fry the slices to heat through.

Serves 4

1.5kg belly pork, cut from the middle

200g granulated sugar

500g coarse sea salt

2 tablespoons chopped thyme

2 tablespoons crushed black peppercorns

melted goose fat or olive oil to cover

For the vegetables:

450g kale

60g unsalted butter

1 tablespoon olive oil

30 baby carrots, peeled

2 tablespoons runny honey

sea salt and black pepper

1 Trim off any bones or excess fat from the pork and cut off any sinew. Mix the sugar and salt with the thyme and peppercorns, then rub into the pork. Cover and leave for at least 2 hours, but preferably overnight, in the fridge. The next day, remove the salt mixture, rinse the meat and pat dry. Cut the skin off with a sharp knife, leaving the fat in place. Roll up the meat like a Swiss roll and tie it tightly in several places with butcher's string.

2 Using a casserole just big enough to hold the pork, add the meat and enough fat or oil to cover it. Place in an oven preheated to 130°C/Gas Mark 1 and cook for about 3½–4 hours, until the meat is very tender: a fork inserted in it should come out with no resistance. Carefully lift it out of the fat (reserving a little for later) and roll it tightly in cling film. Leave to cool, then place in the fridge overnight.

3 Discard the thick stems from the kale and cut the leaves into 2cm strips. Bring a pan of salted water to the boil, add the kale and cook for 5 minutes. Drain, refresh in cold water and drain again.

4 Heat a little of the reserved goose fat in a large frying pan over a medium heat. Unwrap the pork and fry the whole joint to get the outside as crisp as possible – the trick is not to have the heat too high. Place it in an oven preheated to 180°C/Gas Mark 4 and cook for 30 minutes.

5 Meanwhile, melt the butter with the oil in a pan over a medium-low heat. Add the carrots and cook for about 25 minutes until just tender. Stir in the honey, increase the heat, then add the kale and carefully toss all together. Season with salt and pepper. Slice the pork and serve with the vegetables.

CARAMELISED CHICKEN CONFIT STIR-FRY WITH GINGER

In Chinese cuisine, rich meats such as duck are often slow-cooked until they are very well done, yielding a texture similar to confit. It therefore makes sense to use confit in a stir-fry with Chinese flavourings, as in this recipe. Confit of guinea fowl would also be suitable.

Serves 4

4 confit chicken legs (see page 232)

4 tablespoons honey

2 tablespoons soy sauce

30g unsalted butter, melted

For the stir-fry:

2 heads of pak choi

groundnut oil or sesame oil

100g onion, sliced

2 garlic cloves, thinly sliced

1 red pepper, deseeded and thinly sliced

½ long red chilli, thinly sliced

a handful of mangetout, sliced lengthways into 4

1cm piece of fresh ginger, cut into fine strips

8 shiitake mushrooms, stems removed and sliced

2 tablespoons soy sauce

1 teaspoon cornflour

2 teaspoons sugar

sea salt

1 Place the confit chicken legs on a baking tray. Mix the honey, soy sauce and butter together and brush all over the chicken. Place in an oven preheated to 200°C/Gas Mark 6 and cook for 15–20 minutes, basting a couple of times.

2 Cut the pak choi into 6 lengthways, keeping the root attached. Drizzle a large frying pan or wok with the oil and place over a high heat. When hot, add the onion, garlic, red pepper and chilli. Cook for 30 seconds, stirring, then add the mangetout, ginger, mushrooms and pak choi. Cook for 1 more minute, stirring.

3 Put the soy sauce and cornflour into a small bowl and mix to a paste. Add to the pan with the sugar and season with salt. Continue cooking, stirring, for 1 minute on a high heat, then serve with the chicken.

CONFIT OF TUNA WITH SALAD NIÇOISE AND ANCHOVY VINAIGRETTE

Oily fish confit beautifully. It's simply a question of covering them in oil and keeping them at a very low temperature on the hob, but you do need to ensure the heat level stays constant. In a salad niçoise, every ingredient should be seasoned separately, otherwise the salad will be insipid.

Serves 4

2 tuna steaks, weighing about 170g each, cut in half

olive oil

8 quails' eggs

250g small new potatoes

150g French beans, topped and tailed

600g broad beans, shelled

12 baby vine tomatoes

10 anchovy fillets, cut in half lengthways

24 black olives, stoned and cut in half lengthways

16 basil leaves, roughly chopped

2 Little Gem lettuces, leaves separated

fine sea salt and black pepper

For the anchovy vinaigrette:

1 tablespoon very finely chopped shallot

2 anchovy fillets, finely chopped

1 tablespoon lemon juice

6 tablespoons extra virgin olive oil

1 teaspoon sugar

1 Confit the tuna in olive oil the same way as the salmon (see page 236, step 1).

2 Bring a pan of water to the boil, add the quails' eggs and simmer for 2½ minutes, then place them in iced water. Peel off the shells, going round and round the eggs in a spiral shape. Be gentle so as not to damage them.

3 Cook the potatoes in the boiling egg water until just tender. Drain well and cut in quarters lengthways. Season with salt and pepper and set aside

4 Bring more water to the boil in the same pan, add the French beans and cook for about 2 minutes, until tender. Refresh under cold water and drain well. Season with salt and pepper and set aside

5 Cook the broad beans in boiling water for 1 minute, until just tender, then refresh in cold water and peel off the skins. Season with salt and pepper and set aside.

6 Cut the tomatoes in half and put in a bowl, season well with salt and pepper and set aside.

7 To make the vinaigrette, put the shallot in a bowl, add the finely chopped anchovies, lemon juice, olive oil and sugar, then season with salt and pepper.

8 Put the potatoes into a large bowl, add the French beans, broad beans, tomatoes, anchovy fillets, olives and basil leaves. Toss very carefully with your hands, then fold in the lettuce, followed by the anchovy vinaigrette. Divide among serving plates with the cooked quails' eggs and the flaked confit of tuna.

CONFIT OF SALMON WITH CRUSHED POTATOES AND TOMATO AND RED PEPPER SAUCE

When you confit salmon, it turns a wonderful opaque, almost coral colour. You might imagine that the fish would taste oily, but it really doesn't and you wouldn't know it had been cooked in oil at all.

Serves 4

4 salmon fillets, weighing about 140g each, pin bones and skin removed (see page 169, steps 4–7)

extra virgin olive oil or goose fat, to cover

8 black peppercorns

2 teaspoons coriander seeds

2 star anise pods

2 red chillies

1 teaspoon coarse sea salt

finely chopped chives, to garnish

For the sauce:

75ml olive oil

1 shallot, finely chopped

2 garlic cloves, crushed

1 red pepper, skinned (see page 32, step 1), deseeded and roughly chopped

3 tomatoes, skinned (see page 278, step 1), deseeded and chopped

1 teaspoon balsamic vinegar

sea salt and black pepper

For the crushed potatoes:

500g waxy potatoes, such as Charlotte

4 tablespoons olive oil

2 tablespoons snipped chives

1 Before you start, take the salmon out of the fridge and allow it to come up to room temperature. Place a heavy sauté pan or flameproof casserole over a low heat. Add 2–3cm of olive oil or goose fat (enough to cover the salmon) and bring up to no higher than 55°C. Add the peppercorns, coriander seeds, star anise and chillies and allow to infuse for 1 hour. Add the salmon and continue to cook at the same temperature for 20 minutes. If you have the heat too high, you will encourage the fish protein to come out in the form of small white bubbles, which does not look good. When done, the salmon flesh will flake and look opaque but slightly glassy. Remove from the oil, drain it very thoroughly on kitchen paper and sprinkle with the coarse sea salt.

2 Meanwhile, make the sauce. Gently heat 50ml of the olive oil in a pan, add the shallot and cook until softened. Add the garlic, red pepper and tomatoes and season with salt and pepper. Cover and simmer over a low heat for 20 minutes, or until everything is soft, then add the balsamic vinegar. Transfer to a blender and blitz to a fine purée, then stir in the remaining 25ml olive oil and strain. The sauce should coat the back of a spoon; if it is too thick, thin it down with a little water. If you want a very fine-textured sauce, strain it through a fine sieve. Check the seasoning and keep warm.

3 Bring a pan of salted water to the boil, add the potatoes and cook until soft. Drain and return them to the pan to dry out over a low heat. Crush them lightly with a potato masher, then stir in the oil, season with salt and pepper and stir through the chives.

4 Place a small amount of potato on each plate, then top with the salmon. Garnish with chives and serve with the sauce.

CONFIT OF HALIBUT WITH A POTATO AND BACON GALETTE AND BABY TOMATOES

I tend to use extra virgin olive oil to confit fish but you could use goose fat instead. This is the kind of hearty fish dish I really enjoy. Sea bass could be prepared in the same way.

Serves 4

4 halibut steaks or fillets, weighing about 140g each

extra virgin olive oil or goose fat

coarse sea salt

For the potato and bacon galette:

600g potatoes

2 rashers of streaky bacon, finely chopped

100g unsalted butter, plus extra for greasing

1 garlic clove, finely chopped

50g Emmental cheese, finely grated (optional)

sea salt and black pepper

For the baby tomatoes:

20 baby tomatoes, not too ripe

olive oil

grated zest of 1 lime or 1 lemon

1 First make the galette. Slice the potatoes very thinly. Heat a frying pan over a medium-high heat, add the bacon and cook until browned. Take 4 individual 10cm tins or a large gratin dish and grease well with butter. Melt the remaining butter with the garlic and season well with salt and pepper. This should be slightly over-seasoned because the potatoes need a lot of salt, otherwise it will taste bland.

2 Place a layer of potato in the bottom of the dish, then top with some bacon and a little garlic butter, seasoning with salt and pepper between each layer. Make another 2 layers in the same way. Finish with a sprinkling of Emmental cheese, if using. If using individual dishes, place in an oven preheated to 180°C/Gas Mark 4 and cook for 30–35 minutes. If using a large dish, cover and cook for about 1 hour.

3 To make the confit, heat 2–3cm of olive oil or goose fat to 50–55°C. Add the halibut and cook for 30 minutes, as described for the salmon (see page 236, step 1).

4 For the tomatoes, place a double layer of foil in a baking tray. Cut the tomatoes in half, sprinkle with olive oil and the lime or lemon zest, and season with salt and pepper. Bring the foil up over the tomatoes and crimp it across the top to seal. Place in the oven and cook for about 20 minutes, until soft.

5 To serve, place a galette, or slice of galette, on the plate with the halibut and tomatoes, and add a drizzle of juice from the tomatoes.

CONFIT OF SWORDFISH WITH CAPONATA

The Sicilian dish caponata is a real favourite of mine, as it goes with so many things. It is particularly good with rich, oily fish such as swordfish and tuna. The cocoa powder at the end is an unusual touch but it adds a lovely bitter-sweet flavour. I was bowled over when I first tried it.

Serves 4

4 swordfish steaks, weighing about 150g each

extra virgin olive oil

2 teaspoons coriander seeds

3 star anise pods

2 red chillies, deseeded

For the caponata:

100ml olive oil

1 aubergine, diced

½ large red onion, finely diced

1 celery stick, sliced

1 large courgette, finely diced

2 tablespoons capers, rinsed

30g caster sugar

25ml white wine vinegar

50g pine nuts, toasted

200g tomatoes, skinned (see page 278, step 1), deseeded and diced

50g black olives, stoned and halved

2 tablespoons finely chopped flat-leaf parsley

cocoa powder for dusting

sea salt and black pepper

1 First make the caponata. Heat a little of the olive oil in a large frying pan, add the aubergine and cook until browned and soft. You will need to do this in batches. Remove and set aside. In the same frying pan, add more oil and cook the onion and celery without browning, then add the courgette and lightly brown on all sides. Return all the ingredients to the pan, then add the capers, sugar, vinegar, pine nuts, tomatoes, olives and parsley and cook for about 10 minutes. Season with salt and pepper and allow to cool.

2 Make the swordfish confit as described opposite, step 3, using olive oil rather than goose fat. Cook for 30 minutes, then carefully remove from the oil. Serve with the caponata dusted with cocoa powder.

CONFIT OF GARLIC

Confit of garlic cheers up almost any dish. It is particularly wonderful in salads or with fish. It keeps well in a sterilised jar (see page 21) in the fridge, as long as it is completely covered with oil.

4 garlic bulbs

olive oil or goose fat to cover

1 Separate and peel the garlic cloves, then put them in a saucepan with enough oil or goose fat to cover. Heat the oil to 90°C and cook the garlic at this temperature over a low heat for about 1 hour, until soft.

CONFIT OF LEMON

This is so useful to have in your storecupboard for sweet and savoury garnishes. It's also great served with chicken, lamb or guinea fowl. This confit recipe doesn't use fat or oil, instead the lemon is cooked in a sugary solution. Limes and oranges can be prepared in the same way.

3 lemons

150g caster sugar

1 First peel the lemon very finely, taking only the zest and leaving behind any pith. Cut it into very fine strips. Bring a small pan of water to the boil, add the zest for just 10 seconds, then remove and refresh. Repeat twice more, using fresh boiling water and refreshing each time.

2 Put 200ml water and the sugar in a pan and slowly bring to the boil. Add the lemon peel and simmer for 15–20 minutes, until translucent.

CONFIT OF RED ONIONS

Confit of red onion goes with chicken, lamb, fish, sausages — just about anything. You can also make it with shallots. It will keep for a week in the fridge.

4 red onions

30g unsalted butter

30ml oil

1 tablespoon red wine vinegar

150ml red wine

2 tablespoons runny honey

1 rounded teaspoon dried thyme

sea salt and black pepper

1 Cut the onions in half from the stalk to the root. Put the butter and oil into a large sauté pan, add all the onions and cook slowly on both sides until soft. This can take up to 30 minutes.

2 Add the vinegar, red wine and honey and continue cooking until the liquid becomes syrupy, turning the onions frequently. Season with salt and pepper and serve.

PASTA

These days you can buy some very good fresh egg pasta, but it's fun to have a go at making it yourself. People expect making pasta to be complicated, but in fact it's one of the simplest tasks in the kitchen. All you need is one large egg for every 100g flour and that's your pasta. If you are going to make it regularly, I recommend you buy a hand-cranked pasta machine for kneading, rolling and cutting the dough. Making stuffed pasta, such as ravioli or tortellini, is especially satisfying because then you can control the quality of the filling. It's also a very economical way of using up leftovers, such as cooked meat or fish.

I like tagliatelle rather than spaghetti with bolognese sauce, though you can of course use either. If you don't have a pasta machine, see the tips on page 246 for instructions on how to make the tagliatelle with a food processor or by hand. I have used this bolognese recipe for years and it is very reliable. It is slightly drier than some but absolutely delicious.

TAGLIATELLE
with bolognese sauce

To make the pasta dough, follow steps 5 to 10
To make the tagliatelle, follow steps 11 to 15

SERVES 4

2 tablespoons olive oil

1 large onion, finely diced

1 red pepper, skinned (see page 32, step 1), deseeded and very finely chopped

2 celery sticks, cut into 1cm pieces

500g minced beef

2 garlic cloves, finely chopped

200ml red wine

2 bay leaves

400g can of chopped tomatoes

1 tablespoon chopped fresh oregano or ½ teaspoon dried oregano

2 tablespoons tomato purée

a little chicken stock

a pinch of granulated sugar

sea salt and black pepper

chopped parsley, to garnish

freshly grated Parmesan cheese, to serve (optional)

FOR THE PASTA DOUGH:

400g '00' pasta flour, plus extra for dusting

4 eggs

½ teaspoon fine sea salt

1 First make the sauce. Heat the oil in a large sauté pan, add the onion, red pepper and celery and cook gently for about 10 minutes, until softened.

2 Turn the heat up, stir in the minced beef and separate all the strands with 2 forks. Add the garlic and wine and cook for 2 minutes.

3 Add the bay leaves, canned tomatoes and oregano, reduce the heat to low and cook for about 45 minutes, uncovered.

4 Stir in the tomato purée, stock and sugar and season with salt and pepper. Simmer for a further 30 minutes, until a thicker consistency.

5 Meanwhile, to make the pasta dough, put the flour in a mound on a work surface.

6 Make a deep well in the centre by pressing down with the base of a mixing bowl.

7 Add the eggs and salt to the well and mix together with a fork.

8 Using your hands, gradually bring the mixture together and continue mixing until you have a smooth dough. If the mixture is slightly dry, add a little water.

9 Knead the dough lightly on a work surface dusted with pasta flour.

10 Wrap the dough in cling film and leave to rest in the fridge for 30 minutes before rolling out.

11 To make the tagliatelle using a pasta machine, set the rollers on their widest setting and lightly dust with pasta flour.

12 Cut the dough into 8 equal pieces. Flatten each piece in turn into a rectangle and lightly dust with pasta flour.

PASTA

245

13 Feed each rectangle through the rollers 5 times, folding it in half and giving it a half turn after each rolling.

14 Continue feeding the dough through the rollers, narrowing the setting each time but do not fold and turn the dough. Finish at the second-narrowest setting.

15 Once the dough is very thin and smooth, use the tagliatelle cutting attachment on your pasta machine to cut each sheet of dough into ribbons 5mm wide.

16 Cook the tagliatelle immediately in a large saucepan of boiling salted water for 1–2 minutes, until *al dente*.

17 Drain the pasta, then transfer it to a large bowl.

18 Pour the sauce over the tagliatelle and toss well. Garnish with chopped parsley and offer Parmesan cheese for sprinkling.

TIPS AND IDEAS

■ If you are short of time, you can make the pasta dough in a food processor. Put the flour in first, then the eggs and salt and process until it forms crumbs. Tip on to the work surface and press together, adjusting the consistency with a little water or a little more flour if necessary.

■ To make the tagliatelle by hand, cut the pasta dough into 4 pieces. On a lightly floured work surface, roll out each piece in turn as thinly as possible (about 1mm). Keep the dough you aren't working on covered with cling film to prevent it drying out. Loosely fold up each sheet into a narrow rectangle, flouring it if necessary to prevent sticking, then cut it lengthways into ribbons 5mm wide. Lift them up to separate them.

■ A slightly firm pasta dough is preferable to a soft one: it cooks better and gives an *al dente* texture. If you are rolling it out by hand, however, you will be better off with a slightly softer dough so you can get it really thin.

■ Always rest the pasta dough in the fridge to allow the gluten to relax. This makes it easier to roll out. You can leave it for a few hours, if you like, but no longer than 12 as it will discolour slightly. You can freeze it if necessary.

■ To give your pasta a good, rich colour, use eggs from corn-fed chickens, which have bright orange yolks. You can even add a tiny pinch of turmeric to enhance the colour.

■ When the dough is fed through a pasta machine it occasionally tears or sticks. If so, just dust the rollers with a little more flour.

■ If you don't want to cook the tagliatelle immediately, you can hang it over a pole suspended between 2 chairs and leave it to dry for up to 1 hour. After that, coil it up very loosely and leave on a floured tray until you are ready to cook it. If you dry it for longer, it may become brittle, so don't try to coil it.

pasta dough variations

Parsley Pasta Dough – follow the recipe on pages 244–245 to make the pasta dough but add 3 eggs and 3 egg yolks with 2 tablespoons finely chopped flat-leaf parsley and ½ teaspoon fine sea salt to the flour.

Black Olive Pasta Dough – put 12 stoned soft black olives in olive oil in a food processor and process until quite finely puréed. Follow the recipe on pages 244–245 to make the pasta dough but add 3 eggs with the puréed olives and ½ teaspoon fine sea salt to the flour. If the dough is slightly dry, add 1 egg yolk.

Tomato Pasta Dough – follow the recipe on pages 244–245 to make the pasta dough but add 3 eggs with 2 tablespoons tomato purée, 1 garlic clove crushed to a paste with a little salt, 1 teaspoon ground cumin and ½ teaspoon fine sea salt to the flour.

Spinach Pasta Dough – cook 100g fresh spinach in boiling water until just wilted. Drain well and press out any excess liquid. Put into a food processor and process until quite finely puréed. Follow the recipe on pages 244–245 to make the pasta dough but add 3 eggs and 2 egg yolks with the puréed spinach and ½ teaspoon fine sea salt to the flour.

MORE TIPS AND IDEAS

■ If you cut broad ribbons about 2cm wide, you will have pappardelle; fettuccine is usually slightly narrower than tagliatelle, and linguine is narrower still.

■ To make really pretty pasta squares, take a long strip of pasta, rolled out to the second thinnest setting (1mm), put a line of flat-leaf parsley leaves along it, cover with another strip of pasta, then cut the pasta into squares with a leaf in the centre of each one. Roll out on the machine again until you have the required thinness. This is lovely in an open lasagne, perhaps layered with asparagus.

■ Fresh pasta is best eaten on the day it is made.

■ Always cook fresh pasta in lots of boiling salted water – there should be enough room in the pan for it to move freely as it cooks.

■ The sauce should be the correct consistency to coat the pasta rather than swamp it. Add just enough sauce to achieve this, then toss gently until each piece of pasta is lubricated with the sauce.

■ It's worth making some extra pasta so you have it to hand. Roll it out, cover it in cling film, then roll it up loosely and store in plastic bags in the freezer.

FETTUCCINE WITH GUINEA FOWL

Here is a rich and heart-warming pasta dish with a lovely depth of flavour. You can cook this recipe very successfully with duck legs too. Make sure the sauce is nice and thick, so it coats the fettuccine well.

Serves 4

4 guinea fowl legs

30g unsalted butter

50ml olive oil

2 shallots, diced

60g celery, diced

70g carrot, diced

1 leek, thinly sliced

leaves from 2 sprigs of thyme

1 tablespoon tomato purée

2 tablespoons brandy

100ml dry Marsala

250ml chicken stock

juice and grated zest of 1 orange

50g large green olives, stoned and cut into thin strips

1 quantity of Fettuccine (see pages 244–246, but cut into ribbons 4mm wide)

sea salt and black pepper

1 Remove the meat from the guinea fowl legs (see page 44, step 1), then cut it into dice. Melt the butter with the oil in a flameproof casserole, add the meat and cook for 3–4 minutes, until browned, then remove and set aside.

2 Put the shallots, celery, carrot and leek in the casserole and cook for 5–6 minutes, until browned. Stir in the thyme leaves. Dilute the tomato purée with the brandy, then add it to the vegetables along with the Marsala and stock. Return the meat to the casserole, cover and simmer over a low heat for 45 minutes, until tender. Add the orange juice and zest and simmer to reduce a little. Add the olives, cook for a further 15 minutes and season with salt and pepper. The consistency should be thick enough to coat the pasta.

3 Bring a large pan of salted water to the boil, add the fettuccine and cook for 2 minutes. Drain well and serve with the guinea fowl sauce.

SEAFOOD LINGUINE

This will work with any type of pasta ribbons. It's a simple, classic dish that benefits from using really good fresh seafood.

Serves 4

250ml fish stock

500g mussels, cleaned (see page 211)

500g clams, cleaned (see page 211)

extra virgin olive oil

8 langoustines, shelled and deveined (see page 212, step 1)

2 large tomatoes, skinned (see page 278, step 1), deseeded and chopped

2 garlic cloves, chopped

2 tablespoons finely chopped flat-leaf parsley

100ml double cream

300g fresh Linguine (see pages 244–246, but cut into ribbons 2mm wide)

sea salt and black pepper

1 Put the fish stock into a large saucepan, bring to the boil and add the mussels and clams. Cover with a lid and cook until they open, about 4–5 minutes. Discard any that do not open. Remove from the saucepan, then strain the liquid through a sieve lined with muslin, reserving the liquid. Remove the meat from the clams and mussels and set aside.

2 Heat a little oil in a large frying pan. Add the langoustines, cook for 1 minute, then set aside with the mussels. Add the chopped tomatoes to the same pan with the garlic, parsley and strained mussel liquid, bring to the boil, then simmer until reduced and thickened. Season well with salt and pepper. Add the cream and cook for 1 minute, then add the mussels, clams and langoustines.

3 Bring a large pan of salted water to the boil, add the linguine and cook for 3 minutes. Drain well, toss in the sauce and serve.

LINGUINE AND BABY SQUID WITH TOMATO SAUCE

When cooked briefly, as it is here, squid is tender and full of flavour. Pairing it with tomatoes and parsley is a classic combination.

Serves 4

8 baby squid with tentacles

4 tablespoons extra virgin olive oil

1 small onion, finely chopped

4 sundried tomatoes, finely chopped

2 large ripe beef tomatoes, skinned (see page 278, step 1), deseeded and diced

2 bay leaves

300ml fish stock

60g unsalted butter

1 tablespoon chopped rosemary

300g fresh Linguine (see pages 244–246, but cut into ribbons 2mm wide)

2 tablespoons freshly grated Parmesan cheese

2 tablespoons chopped flat-leaf parsley

sea salt and black pepper

1 Prepare the squid as described on page 199, steps 1–10.

2 Heat half the olive oil in a large frying pan, add the onion and cook until softened. Add both lots of tomatoes, the bay leaves and fish stock and cook until the mixture starts to thicken, then remove from the heat and whisk in the butter.

3 In another frying pan, heat the remaining oil over a high heat, add the squid and rosemary and cook for 2 minutes. Season well with salt and pepper, then add the tomato mixture.

4 Bring a large pan of salted water to the boil, add the linguine and cook for 3 minutes, then drain. Add the tomato and squid sauce to the pasta and toss well. Top with the Parmesan and parsley to serve.

SMOKED HADDOCK LASAGNE

Smoked fish with pasta is not traditional but it is wonderful. I've never known anyone not to enjoy this dish.

Serves 6

1 quantity Pasta Dough (see pages 244–245, steps 5–10)

650g undyed smoked haddock fillets

500ml milk

35g unsalted butter, plus extra for greasing

35g plain flour

1 teaspoon freshly grated nutmeg

1 egg yolk

2 tablespoons finely chopped parsley

2 tablespoons finely chopped chives

55g Parmesan cheese, freshly grated

sea salt and black pepper

1 Divide the pasta dough into 4 pieces. Either roll them out by machine (see pages 245–246, steps 11–14) or by hand (see page 246, tips). Keep the dough you aren't working on covered with cling film to prevent it from drying out. Cut the sheets of pasta into wide strips that will fit a large ovenproof dish in which you intend to put the lasagne. Cover the strips with a clean, damp tea towel until you are ready to cook them. Bring a large pan of salted water to the boil, add the pasta and cook for 1 minute. Drain well and place on a clean, damp tea towel without overlapping the strips.

2 Put the haddock in an ovenproof dish and cover with the milk. Place in an oven preheated to 180°C/ Gas Mark 4 and cook for about 10 minutes, until almost cooked. Check it after 5 minutes. Leaving the oven on, remove the dish and set aside for 15 minutes to let the fish settle and the juices ooze out. Reserve the fish and strain the milk.

3 Melt the butter in a saucepan, add the flour and mix to a paste over a low heat, stirring constantly, for 1 minute. Gradually add the strained milk, stirring constantly, until you have a smooth sauce. Add the nutmeg and cook slowly until thick, then season with salt and pepper. Allow the sauce to cool a little, then add the egg yolk.

4 Remove the haddock skin and bones and leave the fish to drain thoroughly in a colander.

5 Butter your lasagne dish. Put a piece of lasagne in the bottom of it, spread with some white sauce, then some haddock, a sprinkling of the parsley and chives, then another layer of sauce. Repeat the sequence until you have 3 layers, finishing with a little sauce on the top. Sprinkle with the Parmesan, then place in the oven and cook for 25–30 minutes, until golden.

SALMON AND PESTO LASAGNE

I've been cooking this for years, and it's a lovely dish to prepare for a large gathering. Fish makes for a much lighter lasagne than meat.

Serves 4–6

1 quantity of Pasta Dough (see pages 244–245, steps 5–10)

600g salmon fillet, skinned

unsalted butter for greasing

1 quantity of Pesto (see page 174)

100g Parmesan cheese, freshly grated

sea salt and black pepper

For the white sauce:

35g unsalted butter

35g plain flour

500ml milk

a pinch of freshly grated nutmeg

sea salt and white pepper

1 Divide the pasta dough into 4 pieces. Either roll them out by machine (see pages 245–246, steps 11–14)or by hand (see page 246, tips). Keep the dough you aren't working on covered with cling film to prevent it from drying out. Cut the sheets of pasta into wide strips that will fit a large ovenproof dish in which you intend to put the lasagne. Cover the strips with a clean, damp tea towel until you are ready to cook them. Bring a large pan of salted water to the boil, add the pasta and cook for 1 minute. Drain well and place on a clean, damp tea towel without overlapping the strips.

2 To make the white sauce, melt the butter in a saucepan, add the flour and mix to a paste over a low heat, stirring constantly, for 1 minute. Gradually add the milk, stirring constantly, until you have a smooth sauce. Add the nutmeg and cook slowly until thick, then season with salt and white pepper. Strain through a fine sieve and allow to cool.

3 Cut the salmon into thin diagonal slices. Butter your lasagne dish, put a piece of lasagne in the bottom of it, brush with some pesto, then place some of the salmon on top, season with salt and pepper, and spread with a little white sauce. Continue making layers in this way, finishing with a layer of white sauce. Sprinkle with the Parmesan, then place in an oven preheated to 180°C/Gas Mark 4 and cook for 30–40 minutes, until golden.

CANNELLONI WITH RICOTTA, MOZZARELLA AND HAM

Including egg in the filling ensures that the cheese sets slightly, which gives an incredibly light cannelloni.

Serves 4

1 quantity of Pasta Dough (see pages 244–245, steps 5–10)

unsalted butter for greasing and dotting

50g Parmesan cheese, freshly grated, plus extra to serve

sea salt and black pepper

For the filling:

200g ricotta cheese

50g Parmesan cheese, freshly grated

1 egg

1 egg yolk

250g ham, diced

150g mozzarella cheese, diced

For the tomato sauce:

2 tablespoons olive oil

500g tomatoes, skinned (see page 278, step 1), deseeded and chopped

8 basil leaves, torn into small pieces

1 Divide the pasta dough into 4 pieces. Either roll them out by machine (see pages 245–246, steps 11–14) or by hand (see page 246, tips). Keep the dough you aren't working on covered with cling film to prevent it from drying out. Cut the sheets into rectangles measuring 12 x 8cm. Cover with a clean, damp tea towel until you are ready to cook.

2 To prepare the filling, mix the ricotta, Parmesan, egg and egg yolk, ham and mozzarella in a bowl and season with salt and pepper.

3 To make the tomato sauce, heat the oil in a saucepan, add the tomatoes and cook gently for 20 minutes. Season with salt and pepper, then stir in the basil.

4 Bring a large pan of salted water to the boil. Add the pasta sheets in batches and cook for 30 seconds. Transfer them to a bowl of iced water, then shake dry and dab with kitchen paper. Arrange the pasta, without overlapping, between sheets of cling film and leave until you are ready to use them.

5 Place the pasta sheets on a clean work surface and spoon a line of filling along the length of each one, then roll up.

6 Butter an ovenproof dish and spread a little of the tomato sauce over the bottom. Place the cannelloni, seam-side down, on the sauce, then cover with the rest of the sauce. Sprinkle with the Parmesan and dot with butter. Place in an oven preheated to 180°C/Gas Mark 4 and cook for 20 minutes. Serve with more grated Parmesan handed separately.

How to make ravioli

1 Generously dust a 12-hole ravioli mould with pasta flour.

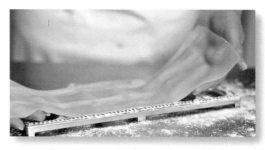

2 Lay a sheet of pasta dough over the mould. Wrap a small ball of the dough in cling film and press it carefully into each hole of the mould to form a depression.

3 Using 2 spoons, place a little of the filling in each hole.

4 Brush the straight edges around each hole with beaten egg or water.

5 Lay a second sheet of pasta dough on top of the filled mould, then run a rolling pin over it to seal the sheets together and cut out the individual parcels.

6 Turn the ravioli out of the mould and make sure each is well sealed. Repeat with the remaining sheets of pasta dough and filling.

If you don't have a ravioli mould, lay a sheet of pasta dough a work surface dusted with pasta flour. Place teaspoonfuls of the filling on it in evenly spaced rows. Brush around the edges of the sheet and between the mounds of filling with beaten egg or water. Lay a second sheet of pasta dough on top and press down around the filling and the edges to seal. Cut between the mounds of filling with a knife or a pastry cutter. Make sure the ravioli are well sealed.

SPINACH AND RICOTTA RAVIOLI WITH RED PEPPER SAUCE

Spinach and ricotta make a lovely light filling. This recipe makes about 40 ravioli. You can make the ravioli, freeze them on an open tray in a single layer, then transfer to a freezer container and store for future use.

Serves 4

400g '00' pasta flour, plus extra for dusting

3 medium eggs,

3 egg yolks

1 tablespoon olive oil

½ teaspoon fine sea salt

1 egg, beaten, to seal

For the spinach and ricotta filling:

30g unsalted butter

450g fresh spinach

125g ricotta cheese

50g Parmesan cheese, freshly grated

3 tablespoons pine nuts, toasted and chopped

1 egg yolk

freshly grated nutmeg

sea salt and black pepper

For the red pepper sauce:

olive oil

1 small onion, finely diced

4 red peppers, skinned (see page 32, step 1) and deseeded

200ml vegetable stock

1 First make the pasta dough as described on page 245, steps 5–10, remembering to add the extra egg yolks, plus the olive oil a bit at a time. You want an eggy, elastic dough, not something greasy.

2 To make the filling, melt the butter in a frying pan, add the spinach and cook for a few minutes, until wilted. Drain well, then pat dry with kitchen paper. Place in a food processor with the ricotta, Parmesan, pine nuts, egg yolk and nutmeg, then pulse briefly so that the mixture retains some texture. Season well with salt and pepper.

3 Divide the pasta dough into 4 pieces. Either roll them out by machine (see pages 245–246, steps 11–14) or by hand (see page 246, tips). Keep the dough you aren't working on covered with cling film to prevent it from drying out. Make the ravioli as described opposite. If not cooking them straight away, leave them in the fridge uncovered.

4 To make the sauce, heat a little oil in a frying pan, add the onion and cook until softened. Transfer to a blender, add the red peppers and blitz to a purée. Pour into a saucepan over a medium heat and add the stock a bit at time, stirring, until you get a sauce consistency. Check the seasoning and keep warm until required.

5 Bring a large pan of salted water to the boil, add the ravioli and cook for 3 minutes. Drain well, then toss with the sauce and serve sprinkled with Parmesan.

WILD MUSHROOM RAVIOLI WITH SAGE CREAM SAUCE

Ravioli can be filled with almost any ingredients you like, so there's nothing to stop you experimenting with your own ideas. The combination used here is particularly good because the earthy flavour of mushrooms goes so well with sage and cream.

Serves 4

400g '00' pasta flour, plus extra for dusting

3 medium eggs

3 egg yolks

1 tablespoon olive oil

½ teaspoon fine sea salt

1 egg, beaten, to seal

For the mushroom filling:

20g dried porcini mushrooms, soaked in boiling water for 30 minutes

150g button mushrooms

1 tablespoon olive oil

1 tablespoon thyme leaves

70g ricotta cheese

1 egg yolk

sea salt and black pepper

For the sage cream sauce:

200ml vegetable stock

300ml double cream

100g Gruyère cheese, finely grated

100g Parmesan cheese, freshly grated

12 sage leaves, finely chopped

1 First make the pasta dough as described on page 245, steps 5–10, remembering to add the extra egg yolks, plus the olive oil a bit at a time. You want an eggy, elastic dough, not something greasy.

2 To make the filling, strain the porcini, reserving the soaking liquid, rinse them well and drain again. Chop the porcini and the fresh mushrooms. Heat the oil in a sauté pan, add all the mushrooms, the strained soaking liquid and thyme and simmer for a few minutes, until tender. Season well with salt and pepper. Transfer to a bowl and leave to cool, then mix in the ricotta and egg yolk.

3 Divide the pasta dough into 4 pieces. Either roll them out by machine (see pages 245–246, steps 11–14) or by hand (see page 246, tips). Keep the dough you aren't working on covered with cling film to prevent it from drying out. Make the ravioli as described on page 256. If not cooking them straight away, leave them in the fridge uncovered.

4 To make the sauce, put the stock and cream into a small saucepan and simmer until reduced by half. Add the Gruyère cheese and half the Parmesan and sage, then leave to infuse while you cook the ravioli.

5 Bring a large pan of salted water to the boil, add the ravioli and cook for 3 minutes. Drain well, then toss with the sauce. Serve sprinkled with the remaining Parmesan and sage.

PASTA

SALMON, PRAWN AND SAFFRON RAVIOLI WITH GINGER SAUCE

Serves 4

a pinch of saffron strands

400g '00' pasta flour, plus extra for dusting

3 medium eggs

3 egg yolks

1 tablespoon olive oil

½ teaspoon fine sea salt

1 egg, beaten, to seal

200g pancetta, fried until crisp, to garnish (optional)

a sprig of chervil, to garnish (optional)

For the filling:

100g salmon fillet, skinned and finely diced

8 raw tiger prawns, peeled (shells reserved), deveined (see page 212, step 1) and roughly chopped

1 teaspoon finely chopped chives

1 teaspoon finely chopped basil

1 teaspoon finely chopped curly parsley

2 tablespoons crème fraîche

sea salt and black pepper

For the sauce:

2 tablespoons olive oil

100g onions, chopped

100g carrots, chopped

4 garlic cloves, chopped

50g fresh ginger, unpeeled, roughly chopped

1 star anise pod

12 basil leaves

2 sprigs of thyme

400ml fish stock

1 tablespoon tomato purée

2 tomatoes, roughly chopped

150ml double cream

a pinch of cayenne

½ teaspoon salt

½ teaspoon sugar

Beurre Manié (see page 70, tips), made with 15g soft unsalted butter and 15g plain flour (optional)

1 Soak the saffron strands in 1 tablespoon of boiling water for 10 minutes. Prepare the pasta dough as described on page 245, steps 5–10, remembering to add the extra egg yolks, plus the olive oil a bit at a time. You want an eggy, elastic dough, not something greasy. When you get to step 7 of making the pasta dough, add the saffron and infused water.

2 Make the filling by putting all the ingredients in a bowl and season well with salt and pepper. Cover and leave in the fridge until required.

3 To make the sauce, heat the oil in a frying pan, add the prawn shells and cook until browned. Add the onions, carrots, garlic, ginger, star anise, basil and thyme and continue cooking for about 4 minutes, until the flavours start to come out. Add the fish stock, tomato purée and tomatoes and bring to the boil. Reduce the heat to a simmer and cook for 20 minutes. Add the cream, bring to the boil again and simmer for a few minutes, then add the cayenne, salt and sugar. Put through a fine strainer, then return the sauce to the cleaned pan. Check the seasoning. If the sauce needs thickening slightly, whisk in a little *beurre manié* a small piece at a time – you may not need it all – and bring back to the boil. Set aside.

4 Divide the pasta dough into 4 pieces. Either roll them out by machine (see pages 245–246, steps 11–14) or by hand (see page 246, tips). Keep the dough you aren't working on covered with cling film to prevent it from drying out. Put the pasta sheets on a lightly floured work surface and cut out equal numbers of circles, half of them 9cm in diameter, the other half about 11cm. Place a rounded tablespoon of the filling in the centre of each small circle. Brush around it with beaten egg, then place a larger pasta circle on top and seal the edges very well all around.

5 Bring a large pan of salted water to the boil, add the ravioli and cook for 5 minutes. Serve with the sauce and garnish with the pancetta and chervil, if using.

BUTTERNUT SQUASH TORTELLINI WITH CRUSHED AMARETTI

Serves 4

400g '00' pasta flour, plus extra for dusting

3 medium eggs

3 egg yolks

2 tablespoons olive oil

½ teaspoon fine sea salt

1 egg, beaten, to seal

For the filling:

300g butternut squash, deseeded

3 tablespoons pine nuts, toasted

1 egg yolk

50g ricotta cheese

12 amaretti biscuits, crushed to a powder

1 tablespoon chopped sage

2 tablespoons freshly grated Parmesan cheese

sea salt and black pepper

For the sauce:

60g unsalted butter

30g shallots, finely diced

1 garlic clove, finely chopped

200g butternut squash, peeled and cut into
1cm dice

50ml sherry

300ml vegetable stock

a pinch of cayenne pepper

100ml double cream

1 Prepare the pasta dough as described on page 245, steps 5–10, remembering to add the extra egg yolks, plus the olive oil a bit at a time. You want an eggy, elastic dough, not something greasy.

2 To make the filling, cut the butternut squash into 3cm slices and put on a baking tray. Place in an oven preheated to 180°C/Gas Mark 4 and cook for 1 hour, until soft. Allow to cool, then peel, put the flesh into a food processor and blitz until smooth. Transfer it to a non-stick frying pan over a low heat and cook gently to evaporate the liquid: it should be very dry

but not brown. Allow it to cool, then place in a large bowl. Chop 2 tablespoons of the pine nuts and add them to the squash, along with the egg yolk, ricotta, amaretti and sage, and season generously with salt and pepper. Stir well and finally add the Parmesan.

3 To make the tortellini, roll out the dough as described on pages 245–246, steps 11–14, then cut the sheets in half lengthways. Put half-teaspoons of the filling along each strip, leaving a 3cm gap between each mound. Cut between them to form squares. Brush a little beaten egg around the filling, then fold the pasta corner to corner, making sure you get all the air out of each piece and sealing well. Flip the top of the triangle towards you, then bring the 2 bottom corners together; twist and seal to make a tortellini shape. Put on a floured tray and refrigerate until ready to cook.

4 To make the sauce, heat a little butter in a large frying pan, add the shallots and garlic and cook until softened. Add the squash, cook gently for 5 minutes, to soften, then add the sherry and cook for a further 5 minutes, stirring to dislodge any sediment in the bottom of the pan. Add the stock and simmer for about 25 minutes. Season well with salt and pepper and add the cayenne. Strain through a fine sieve, reserving the liquid. Purée the squash in a blender, add half of it to the liquid and stir well. Continue to add the squash until you have a medium-thick sauce. Add the cream, check the seasoning and keep warm until required.

5 Bring a large pan of salted water to the boil, add the tortellini and cook for 3 minutes, then drain. Serve with the sauce and sprinkle with the remaining pine nuts.

POLENTA

Polenta is one of those things that people either love or hate. I have had good polenta and bad polenta, but if you've had a bad experience with it, please don't be put off. Cooked properly, it is heavenly. Most recipes will tell you to make it with water but I always use stock, which means the end result is so much more flavoursome. It's also a very good idea to add some cheese for extra interest.

Creamed polenta is a soft mixture that has to be served pretty much straight after cooking, otherwise it will set. Here it is accompanied by pork chops but it also goes well with chicken or sausages. It takes no more than 15 minutes to make, so is a perfect fast food — and a good alternative to reaching for the pasta every time.

SEARED PORK CHOPS

with creamed polenta

To make the creamed polenta, follow steps 1 to 4

SERVES 4

4 large pork chops, weighing about 220–250g each

2 tablespoons olive oil

75g unsalted butter

1 tablespoon redcurrant jelly

100ml chicken stock

sea salt and black pepper

4 sprigs of rosemary, to garnish

FOR THE CREAMED POLENTA:

500ml chicken stock, plus a little extra if needed

125ml full-fat milk

125g polenta

75g unsalted butter, diced

100g Gruyère cheese, grated

150ml double cream

1 First make the creamed polenta. Bring the stock and milk to the boil in a large saucepan.

2 Reduce the heat to a simmer and gradually sprinkle in the polenta, whisking constantly with a balloon whisk until completely smooth.

3 Continue cooking gently for about 10 minutes, whisking constantly.

4 Add the butter and Gruyère, mix well, then season with salt and pepper. Set the polenta aside while you cook the chops.

5 Season the pork chops on both sides with salt and pepper. Place a heavy-based frying pan over a medium-high heat and, when it's hot, add the oil.

6 Add the chops, reduce the heat to medium and cook for 4–5 minutes on each side until firm, basting with 35g of the butter.

7 Transfer the chops to a plate and keep warm.

8 Put the remaining 40g butter in the pan along with the redcurrant jelly and stock, bring to the boil and cook for 1 minute, until the mixture starts to thicken slightly.

9 Heat the polenta through while whisking in the cream and a little more stock to make it smooth. Check the seasoning again. Serve each chop with a spoonful of the creamed polenta garnished with a sprig of rosemary and some of the sauce poured around it.

POLENTA

TIPS AND IDEAS

■ In the recipe on pages 264–265 the polenta is cooked in a combination of milk and stock. The milk makes it a little creamier, but you could use stock alone if you prefer.

■ I always buy the quick-cooking polenta, which takes only about 10 minutes to make.

■ Always sprinkle the polenta very slowly into the hot liquid, otherwise lumps will form.

■ The polenta is cooked when it pulls away from the side of the pan.

■ Because it is so bland, polenta must be seasoned very generously indeed.

■ Leftover polenta can be allowed to set, then sliced and either grilled or fried, as described on page 268, step 5.

■ Soft polenta goes with virtually anything you would serve with mashed potatoes.

■ Set polenta can be cut into any shape you like using biscuit cutters. Hearts look lovely, or you can cut someone's initials. Serving 'shaped' food is a nice way of encouraging children to eat polenta.

polenta variations

Polenta with Herbs – make the polenta as on pages 264–265, finely chopping a large handful of herbs and stirring it into the boiling stock and milk with the polenta. Parsley, basil, sage or a mixture of all three work well.

Polenta with Pesto – make the polenta as on pages 264–265, stirring 3 tablespoons pesto into the cooked polenta.

Black Olive and Rosemary Polenta – make the polenta as on pages 264–265, stirring 3 tablespoons finely chopped black olives and 1 teaspoon finely chopped rosemary into the cooked polenta.

Saffron Polenta – make the polenta as on pages 264–265, adding a good pinch of saffron strands to the boiling stock.

Polenta with Red Pepper – roast a large red pepper and peel off the skin (see page 32, step 1), then deseed and dice it. Make the polenta as on pages 264–265, stirring the roasted pepper into the cooked polenta.

FRIED SAFFRON POLENTA WITH SPINACH AND FRIED EGG

This makes a wonderful alternative to eggs Benedict, with polenta taking the place of toasted muffins. It's a real treat, particularly for anyone who has to follow a gluten-free diet.

Serves 4

1 quantity of Saffron Polenta (see page 267), omitting the butter, Gruyère cheese and double cream

1 tablespoon olive oil, plus a drizzle

100g unsalted butter

300g fresh spinach

4 large very fresh eggs

sea salt and black pepper

For the hollandaise sauce:

250g unsalted butter

2 tablespoons white wine vinegar

2 tablespoons water

1 bay leaf

1 teaspoon white peppercorns

4 egg yolks

juice of 1 lemon, or to taste

sea salt and white pepper

1 Pour the saffron polenta into a small baking tray and spread evenly. Cover with cling film and leave to cool, then place in the fridge for a couple of hours to firm up.

2 Meanwhile, to make the hollandaise sauce, first clarify the butter. Melt the butter in a small, heavy-based saucepan over a very low heat until the milky residue has separated. Skim off any froth from the top, pour the clear butter into a jug and leave to cool slightly. Discard the residue in the pan.

3 Put the vinegar, water, bay leaf and peppercorns into another small, heavy-based saucepan, bring to the boil and cook until reduced to 1 tablespoon. Strain the liquid into a bowl and leave to cool slightly.

4 Set a heatproof bowl over a saucepan of simmering water, making sure the water doesn't touch the base of the bowl. Pour the reduction into the bowl and turn off the heat. Lightly whisk the egg yolks, add them to the reduction and stir until they start to thicken slightly to a cream. Very slowly pour in the clarified butter, whisking constantly with a balloon whisk. If the mixture becomes too thick, warm briefly over a low heat but make sure it doesn't overheat. Stir in the lemon juice and season well with salt and white pepper. Leave the sauce in the bowl over the pan of hot water.

5 Cut the polenta into 4 squares. Heat a drizzle of olive oil in a large frying pan, add the polenta squares and cook over a medium heat for about 3 minutes on each side until browned – keeping the heat down will ensure a golden crust.

6 Meanwhile, melt 75g of the butter in a large frying pan, add the spinach and cook, stirring, until wilted. Season generously with salt and pepper, then drain well.

7 Wipe the pan out, add the remaining 25g butter and melt with the 1 tablespoon oil. Crack the eggs one by one into a cup, then gently slide into the frying pan. Cook over a low heat for about 3 minutes, until done to your liking.

8 To serve, place a piece of polenta in the centre of each plate, top with some spinach and a fried egg and pour over the hollandaise sauce.

TOMATO, AUBERGINE AND GRUYÈRE TART WITH POLENTA PASTRY

Polenta pastry is remarkably easy to handle and has a lovely texture and colour.

Makes 4 individual tarts

100ml olive oil

1 aubergine, finely diced

sea salt and black pepper

For the polenta pastry:

100g plain flour, plus extra for dusting

40g polenta

60g cold unsalted butter, cut into small cubes

15g Parmesan cheese, freshly grated

1 egg, lightly beaten

1 teaspoon fine sea salt

¼ teaspoon cayenne pepper

For the tomato and cheese topping:

2 tablespoons olive oil

2 shallots, finely chopped

2 garlic cloves, finely chopped

8 large tomatoes (not beef tomatoes), skinned (see page 278, step 1) and deseeded

2 sprigs of thyme, finely chopped

a sprig of rosemary, finely chopped

1 tablespoon tomato purée

1 teaspoon granulated sugar

150g Gruyère or Cheddar cheese, finely grated

1 First make the polenta pastry. Sift the flour and polenta into a bowl and mix together. Add the butter and rub in with your fingertips until the mixture resembles fine breadcrumbs. Stir in the Parmesan, then add the egg, salt and cayenne. Mix with a round-bladed knife or a fork, then use your hands to form it into a dough. Knead lightly until smooth. Wrap in cling film and leave to rest in the fridge for 30 minutes.

2 Roll out the pastry on a lightly floured work surface until 2mm thick, then cut out four 14cm circles. Use to line four 10cm tart tins, making sure the pastry fits snugly. Prick the bases lightly with a fork. Scrunch up 4 pieces of baking parchment, then unfold and use to line the pastry cases. Fill right up to the top with baking beans, rice or dried beans. Place the tins on a hot baking sheet in an oven preheated to 190°C/ Gas Mark 5 and bake for 15–20 minutes, until pale golden. Remove the paper and beans or rice, then return the tins to the oven for 5 minutes, until the pastry is dry and lightly coloured. Remove from the oven and leave to cool in the tins.

3 For the filling, heat the oil in a heavy-based frying pan, add the aubergine and cook until browned all over. Transfer to a sieve and leave to drain, then season well with salt and pepper. Wipe out the pan.

4 For the topping, heat the oil in the frying pan, add the shallots and garlic and cook until softened. Add the tomatoes with the herbs and cook until soft and all the liquid has evaporated. Stir in the tomato purée and sugar and season well with salt and pepper.

5 To assemble the tarts, divide the aubergine between the pastry cases, then top with the tomato mixture and the cheese. Place in an oven preheated to 200°C/ Gas Mark 6 and bake for 10 minutes – if the tops need further browning, place under a preheated grill for a few minutes.

GREEN OLIVE BREAD WITH POLENTA

*Here a simple bread dough is coated in dry polenta, then cut into squares to make rolls.
Serve warm, with olive oil for dipping.*

Makes 10 rolls

500g strong white flour, plus extra for dusting

15g fresh yeast (or a 7g sachet of dried easy-blend yeast)

300ml tepid water

45ml olive oil

1 teaspoon fine sea salt

6 tablespoons pimento-stuffed green olives, chopped

75g polenta

1 Put the flour into a bowl, crumble in the fresh yeast (or stir in the easy-blend yeast) and mix well. Add the tepid water and oil and stir until the mixture begins to form a dough.

2 Turn the dough on to a work surface and knead firmly. To do this, hold the dough down at the front with the fingers of one hand, push the rest of it with the palm of your other hand to stretch it, then roll the dough up and give it a quarter turn. Your hands will become sticky, so dip them regularly into a bowl of flour and clap them to shake off the excess. Knead the dough for 7 minutes, until it begins to feel elastic, then sprinkle over the salt and continue kneading for another 7 minutes. Add the olives to the dough and knead again until they are well incorporated.

3 Line a 24–35cm round cake tin with a clean cloth and flour it really well. Roll out the dough into a circle about 2cm thick. Place it on the floured cloth and sprinkle water over the top. Scatter with polenta, patting it all over the dough. Cover with another clean cloth and leave to rise at room temperature for about 1 hour, or until it has doubled in size.

4 Carefully turn the dough out on to a floured board. Using a floured knife, cut the dough into lengths and then into squares so you end up with 10 pieces. Carefully flip them polenta-side up, arrange them spaced apart on a baking sheet and leave to rise, uncovered, for a few minutes more.

5 Place in an oven preheated to 220°C/Gas Mark 7 and bake for about 10 minutes, until the rolls sound hollow when tapped underneath.

GNOCCHI

Gnocchi are little Italian potato dumplings that are cooked in a large pan of boiling water like pasta. Homemade gnocchi are a world away from the ones you buy pre-packed — there is absolutely no comparison whatsoever. In Italy, gnocchi are usually served on their own as a first course, but I also like them as an accompaniment. You can add virtually any flavouring you like and they are perfect for vegetarians.

Blue cheese and walnuts are a classic combination and make a lovely foil for fresh gnocchi. After boiling, the gnocchi are baked with the sauce poured over them. You can assemble the dish well in advance and bake at the last minute.

POTATO GNOCCHI
with Gorgonzola sauce and walnuts

To make the potato gnocchi, follow steps 1 to 6

SERVES 6

700g medium red potatoes, washed

100g Parmesan cheese, freshly grated

80g walnuts, finely chopped, plus 50g whole walnut halves to garnish

¼ teaspoon freshly grated nutmeg

150g plain flour, plus 100g for dusting

sea salt and white pepper

FOR THE GORGONZOLA SAUCE:

500ml full-fat milk

2 bay leaves

½ onion

6 white peppercorns

a sprig of thyme

40g unsalted butter

40g plain flour

100ml double cream

150g Gorgonzola cheese, crumbled

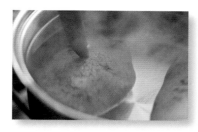

1 Cook the whole unpeeled potatoes in a large saucepan of boiling salted water for about 20–25 minutes, or until a knife inserted into them comes out easily.

2 Drain and leave until cool enough to handle. Peel off the skins, then leave the potatoes in a colander to dry off for a few minutes.

3 Pass the potatoes through a potato ricer into a bowl.

4 Add 50g of the Parmesan, the finely chopped walnuts, nutmeg and flour and season with salt and white pepper. Mix together well.

5 Divide the mixture into 6 pieces. Roll each piece into a sausage as thick as your little finger. Cut each roll into 2cm lengths and dust with flour.

6 Press the cut side of each piece on to the tines of a fork with your thumb.

7 To make the sauce, pour the milk into a saucepan and add the bay leaves, onion, white peppercorns and thyme. Bring slowly to simmering point.

8 Remove from the heat and leave to infuse for at least 20 minutes, but preferably overnight. Strain the infused milk into a jug.

9 Gently melt the butter in a heavy-based saucepan. Add the flour and cook, stirring, over a low heat for 1 minute without browning.

10 Gradually add the infused milk, stirring constantly with a wooden spoon.

11 Make sure the mixture is smooth and well blended each time before you make the next addition.

12 When all the milk has been added, continue stirring until the mixture is smooth and silky. Bring to the boil, then simmer over a low heat for 2 minutes.

13 Stir in the cream and Gorgonzola and season with white pepper and a little salt – taste before adding the latter as the cheese is already salty.

14 Transfer the sauce to a bowl and set over a saucepan of hot water to keep warm while you cook the gnocchi.

15 Bring a large saucepan of salted water to a simmer. Drop a few gnocchi at a time into the water.

16 Simmer gently for 1 minute, until they rise to the surface. Remove the gnocchi with a slotted spoon, put them on to a tray and leave to cool.

17 Transfer all the gnocchi to individual gratin dishes and pour over the sauce.

18 Top with the walnut halves and sprinkle over the remaining 50g Parmesan. Place in an oven preheated to 180°C/Gas Mark 4 and bake for 20 minutes. Serve straight away.

TIPS AND IDEAS

■ Floury potato varieties, such as Desirée and Maris Piper, are best for gnocchi.

■ After peeling the cooked potatoes, make sure they are as dry as possible before making the gnocchi, otherwise the mixture will be too wet.

■ If you don't have a potato ricer, you can push the potatoes through a sieve.

■ It is important to form the gnocchi while the mixture is still warm.

■ Marking the gnocchi with a fork helps them to cook more evenly.

■ When you drop the gnocchi into the water, don't worry that they will disintegrate. As long as you keep the heat at a gentle simmer, they will miraculously rise to the top.

■ Always serve gnocchi with masses of sauce – it should be a rich, indulgent dish. I sometimes double the quantities given on page 274.

potato gnocchi variations

Spinach Gnocchi – cook and sieve 450g potatoes as described on page 275, steps 1–3. Cook 500g fresh spinach in a little water until wilted, then drain and press out all the liquid so it is as dry as possible. Whiz to a purée in a food processor. Transfer to a bowl and mix with 75g ricotta cheese, 100g freshly grated Parmesan cheese, 100g plain flour, the potato, 1 teaspoon freshly grated nutmeg and some salt and pepper. Roll, shape and cook the gnocchi as described on pages 275–276). Bake covered in a Béchamel sauce (see opposite), with a little grated Parmesan sprinkled on top.

Black Olive Gnocchi – follow the recipe on pages 274–275, replacing the walnuts and nutmeg with 150g stoned black olives, very finely chopped.

Basil Gnocchi – follow the recipe on pages 274–275, replacing the walnuts with a large handful of chopped basil.

HERB GNOCCHI WITH TOMATO SAUCE

These are lovely, light, summery gnocchi. Use whatever herbs you can lay your hands on.

Serves 6

1 quantity of Potato Gnocchi (see pages 274–275), but add a large handful of chopped herbs, such as parsley, chervil, chives and/or thyme, and omit the walnuts

freshly grated Parmesan, to serve

For the tomato sauce:

1kg ripe but firm tomatoes

4 tablespoons olive oil

1 small onion, finely chopped

2 garlic cloves, finely chopped

1 teaspoon dried oregano

1 tablespoon tomato purée

1 teaspoon granulated sugar

sea salt and black pepper

1 First make the sauce. To skin the tomatoes, score a cross on the top of each one, place in boiling water for 25 seconds, then transfer to a bowl of iced water. The skin should peel off easily. Cut each tomato into quarters, discard the seeds and roughly chop the flesh.

2 Heat the oil in a large, heavy-based frying pan, add the onion and cook gently until soft but not coloured. Stir in the garlic, tomatoes and oregano. Bring to a simmer and cook over a medium heat until the sauce starts to thicken. Stir in the tomato purée and sugar, season with salt and pepper and cook for a further 2 minutes.

3 Cook the gnocchi as described on page 276, steps 15–16. Serve with the sauce spooned over the top and generously sprinkled with Parmesan.

POTATO GNOCCHI WITH TALEGGIO, SAGE AND CARROTS

Taleggio is a lovely cheese for melting. Be careful not to overdo the sage, as the flavour can overpower the other ingredients.

Serves 6

1 tablespoon olive oil

250g carrots, peeled and cut into fine strips

1 tablespoon chopped sage leaves

100ml double cream

150g Taleggio cheese, diced

1 tablespoon dried sage

1 quantity of Potato Gnocchi (see pages 274–275), but add 1 tablespoon dried sage and omit the walnuts

sea salt and white pepper

4 sprigs of sage, to garnish

For the béchamel sauce:

500ml full-fat milk

2 bay leaves

½ onion

6 white peppercorns

a sprig of thyme

40g unsalted butter

40g plain flour

1 Heat the oil in a frying pan, add the carrots and the fresh sage and cook until softened. Remove from the heat and leave to cool.

2 To make the béchamel sauce, pour the milk into a saucepan and add the bay leaves, onion, peppercorns and thyme. Bring slowly to a simmer, then remove from the heat and leave to infuse for as long as possible. Strain the infused milk through a sieve into a jug. Melt the butter gently in a heavy-based saucepan. Add the flour and cook, stirring, over a low heat for 1 minute, without browning. Gradually add the infused milk, stirring constantly with a wooden spoon, making sure the mixture is smooth before you make the next addition. Continue stirring until you have a smooth, silky consistency. Bring to the boil, then simmer over a low heat for 2 minutes.

3 Finish the sauce by stirring in the cream, Taleggio and dried sage, and season with salt and white pepper. Transfer the sauce to a bowl and set over a saucepan of hot water to keep warm.

4 Cook the gnocchi as described on page 276, steps 15–16, then leave to cool. Arrange half the carrots in the base of a large gratin dish, add the gnocchi, then sprinkle over the remaining carrots. Pour over the sauce, place in an oven preheated to 180°C/Gas Mark 4 and bake for 20 minutes. Serve garnished with the sprigs of sage.

FRIED HERB GNOCCHI WITH RACK OF LAMB

Fried gnocchi make a delightful alternative to potatoes as an accompaniment to lamb. I tend to make the gnocchi slightly bigger if I am frying them — they just seem to work better that way.

Serves 4

½ quantity of Potato Gnocchi (see pages 274–275), but add a small handful of chopped herbs, such as parsley, chervil, chives and/or thyme, and omit the walnuts

a drizzle of olive oil

4 three-rib racks of lamb, French-trimmed

sea salt and black pepper

a few pea shoots, to garnish

For the sauce:

a drizzle of olive oil

1kg lamb bones

150g onions, finely chopped

2 garlic cloves, finely chopped

2 tomatoes

1 tablespoon redcurrant jelly

2 sprigs of thyme

chicken stock or water, to cover

For the lamb coating:

100g dried white breadcrumbs

2 anchovy fillets, finely chopped

4 tablespoons finely chopped parsley

1 tablespoon thyme leaves

1 tablespoon finely chopped rosemary

2 garlic cloves, finely chopped

4 teaspoons Dijon mustard

1 Cook the gnocchi as described on page 276, steps 15–16, then leave to cool.

2 To make the sauce, heat the oil in a large saucepan, add the bones and cook until browned on all sides. Add the onion and garlic and cook until browned, then add the tomatoes, redcurrant jelly and thyme. Pour in enough stock or water to cover the bones, bring to the boil, then simmer for about 1 hour, until reduced – you might have to cook and reduce the liquid further to intensify the flavour. Strain through a fine sieve into a saucepan.

3 To finish preparing the gnocchi, heat a drizzle of oil in a large frying pan, add a batch of the gnocchi and cook gently until browned on all sides. Set aside and cook the remaining gnocchi in the same way. (You can do this several hours in advance and reheat the gnocchi in a hot oven when you are ready to serve.)

4 For the lamb coating, put all the ingredients except the mustard into a food processor, season with salt and pepper and process until well combined.

5 Skin the racks of lamb, keeping as much fat on them as possible. Heat a drizzle of oil in a large frying pan, add the racks, fat-side down, and cook for about 2 minutes. Transfer to a large roasting tray, fat-side up, place in an oven preheated to 190°C/ Gas Mark 5 and cook for 10 minutes. Season with pepper and set aside to cool. Brush a teaspoon of the mustard on to each rack, then press the coating down over the mustard (not on the bones), making it as neat as possible. Return to the oven for a further 8–10 minutes.

6 Meanwhile, finish the sauce by seasoning it with salt and pepper and reducing it a little further.

7 Remove the lamb from the oven and leave to rest for 5 minutes. Meanwhile, reheat the gnocchi in the oven if necessary. Carve each rack into separate ribs and arrange in the centre of each serving plate. Surround with the gnocchi, garnished with pea shoots, and with the sauce spooned around.

INDEX

ACKNOWLEDGEMENTS

Author's acknowledgements

I would like to thank a number of people who have helped me with this book – I could not have done it without them.

Thank you to my recipe testers: chef Stephanie Moon, who helped test almost every recipe with good humour and total dedication; the lovely Stephanie Welford, who did endless washing up during the testing process (she was heavily pregnant at the time and gave birth to Ebony-May just two weeks later); and Gillian Fieldhouse, who also helped test a few recipies.

Thank you to my editors: Jane Middleton, who has the patience of a saint and always understands what I am saying; Jo Richardson, who started the book off; Laura Gladwin, who never gave up trying to pin me down; and Trish Burgess, was also very patient.

For the photography and design, thank you to Karen Taylor and Chris Taylor, my home economists, for their hard work at the shoot – you did an amazing job; Cristian Barnett for the wonderful photographs – I loved your patience and good humour; Jane Ellis for supervising the shoot; and Miranda Harvey for her art direction and design – you did a fabulous job.

Thank you to the Octopus team: Stephanie Jackson, who totally believed in what I was doing; the ever-thoughtful and kind Stephanie Milner; Clare Churly – thank you for never showing me when you were rattled, you always keep me calm; Jonathan Christie; and Lucy Carter.

I would also like to thank some local food suppliers: Rogers Butchers for helping me with all that curing – I could not have done it without your help; Delifresh for delivering to the house and all the great food; R & J Butchers for the last-minute deliveries; and Carricks for getting the wonderful fish to me on time.

Last, but not least, thank you to my lovely agent, Healther Holden-Brown; thank you to Belinda Wallace for having mountains of patience with me and for typing up all those hundreds of illegible recipies; and thank you to Gilly for doing things for me on occasion so that I could get on with the book.

Publisher's acknowledgements

Thank you to the following companies for lending equipment for the photo shoot: All-Clad (www.all-clad.co.uk), whose pans Rosemary uses at her cookery school at Swinton Park; Wüsthof Knives – UK Contact (www.inthehaus.co.uk); Lakeland (www.lakeland.co.uk) for supplying a range of quality kitchen equipment; and Kenwood (www.kenwoodworld.com/uk) for loaning a Kenwood Chef Titanium with mincer attachment.

Publishing Director: Stephanie Jackson
Managing Editor: Clare Churly
Contributing Editor: Jane Middleton
Art Director: Jonathan Christie
Designer: Miranda Harvey
Photographer: Cristian Barnett
Home Economist: Karen Taylor
Home Economist's Assistant: Chris Taylor
Senior Production Controller: Lucy Carter

Note

A few recipes contain nuts and nut derivatives. Anyone with a known nut allergy must avoid these.

This book contains some dishes made with raw or lightly cooked eggs. It is prudent for more vulnerable people such as pregnant and nursing mothers, invalids, the elderly, babies and young children to avoid raw or lightly cooked eggs.